Praise for
What to Do When You Feel Broken

'*Trauma doesn't have to be the end of your story – it can be the beginning of a new, stronger chapter.* What to Do When You Feel Broken *dives deep into the transformative process known as Post-Traumatic Growth (PTG), revealing how even life's most challenging moments can fuel your resilience, strength, and growth.*'

MEL ROBBINS, BEST-SELLING AUTHOR AND HOST OF *THE MEL ROBBINS PODCAST*

'What to Do When You Feel Broken *is an essential guide for anyone navigating the toughest moments in life. With deep compassion and practical wisdom, this book provides a powerful roadmap for healing. It doesn't just offer fleeting comfort; it equips you with the tools to rebuild your life, piece by piece, from the inside out. Dr. Laura understands the complexity of human emotion, showing how vulnerability and the feeling of 'brokenness' can be transformed into strength. If you've ever felt overwhelmed, lost, or unsure of how to move forward, this book will remind you that even in the darkest times, there is a way forward – one step at a time. An indispensable read for those ready to reclaim their wholeness and truly step into their power.*'

DR. LALITAA SUGLANI, AWARD-WINNING PSYCHOLOGIST
AND AUTHOR OF *HIGH-FUNCTIONING ANXIETY*

'*This is is a wonderful guide to help us better understand ourselves. It shows us how to gain insight into how we think, communicate, and act, and it gives us the tools we need to grow from, and through, the difficult periods in our lives. A highly important and valuable book.*'

DAVID R HAMILTON, PH.D.,
AUTHOR OF *THE JOY OF ACTUALLY GIVING A F*CK*

T0355891

'The practical tools in this book, along with Dr. Laura's personal story and professional qualifications make it the perfect "go to" for advice when one hits life's inevitable moments of adversity. You will be reaching for this book over and over again.'

SIMONE HENG, AWARD-WINNING AUTHOR OF
LET'S TALK ABOUT LONELINESS

'This is such a powerful book. It combines Dr. Laura's own devastating experience of trauma with her many years of clinical practice. She weaves together personal narratives, the research evidence and practical tips, and reflections with such ease and insight. Everyone should read this book; there is something in it for all of us.'

PROFESSOR RORY O'CONNOR, INTERNATIONAL EXPERT IN SUICIDE
PREVENTION AND AUTHOR OF WHEN IT IS DARKEST

'In this excellent, beautifully written book, Dr. Williams skillfully integrates psychological research, clinical expertise, and her own experience of personal loss for clients struggling with the effects of trauma. I was deeply moved by its honesty, and the message that even the most painful, devastating experiences can ultimately help us to live meaningful and more authentic lives.'

PROFESSOR TONY WARD, DIPCLINPSYC, PHD FRSNZ,
CREATOR OF THE GOOD LIVES MODEL

'The powerful combination of professional psychology insights and Dr. Laura's personal story provides the reflections and tools to guide you gently through tough times.'

DR. EMMA HEPBURN (THE PSYCHOLOGY MUM), CLINICAL PSYCHOLOGIST AND AUTHOR

'Dr. Laura generously shares her personal journey through catastrophic loss, offering readers a compassionate guide through key psychological concepts used in therapy. This book is an insightful companion for anyone navigating their own healing process.'

DR. CLAIRE PLUMBLY, CLINICAL PSYCHOLOGIST AND AUTHOR OF BURNOUT

What to Do
When You
Feel Broken

What to Do When You Feel Broken

How to **Let Go** of Negative Patterns,
Heal Your Relationships and
Find Freedom

Dr Laura Williams

HAY HOUSE

Carlsbad, California • New York City
London • Sydney • New Delhi

Published in the United Kingdom by:
Hay House UK Ltd, 1st Floor, Crawford Corner,
91–93 Baker Street, London W1U 6QQ
Tel: +44 (0)20 3927 7290 www.hayhouse.co.uk

Published in the United States of America by:
Hay House LLC, PO Box 5100, Carlsbad, CA 92018-5100
Tel: (1) 760 431 7695 or (800) 654 5126; www.hayhouse.com

Published in Australia by:
Hay House Australia Publishing Pty Ltd, 18/36 Ralph St,
Alexandria NSW 2015 Tel: (61) 2 9669 4299; www.hayhouse.com.au

Published in India by:
Hay House Publishers (India) Pvt Ltd, Muskaan Complex,
Plot No.3, B-2, Vasant Kunj, New Delhi 110 070
Tel: (91) 11 4176 1620; www.hayhouse.co.in

Text © Dr. Laura Williams, 2025

The moral rights of the author have been asserted.

This book features case studies that have been included with the consent of the individuals involved. All names and identifying details have been altered to protect privacy. Any resemblance to actual persons or events is purely coincidental.

The information given in this book should not be treated as a substitute for professional medical advice; always consult a medical practitioner. Any use of information in this book is at the reader's discretion and risk. Neither the author nor the publisher can be held responsible for any loss, claim or damage arising out of the use, or misuse, of the suggestions made, the failure to take medical advice or for any material on third-party websites.

A catalogue record for this book is available from the British Library.

Tradepaper ISBN: 978-1-4019-7900-3
E-book ISBN: 978-1-83782-264-5
Audiobook ISBN: 978-1-83782-263-8

10 9 8 7 6 5 4 3 2 1

Printed in the United States of America

This product uses responsibly sourced papers and/or recycled materials. For more information, see www.hayhouse.com.

For Mum and Dad, who always
believed I was good enough.

Contents

Introduction

When I set out to write this book, the title wasn't 'What to Do When You Feel Broken.' Then, serendipitously, I came across the title of an online workshop I'd run a few years beforehand. It was called 'You Are Not Broken' and it was my most popular online event. The content of that workshop was the beginning of this book, but I just didn't know it back then. I think the event was popular because it talked to a secret fear many of us hold about ourselves: That all we've been through, and all the mistakes we've made along the way, mean we are in fact broken. Shattered, damaged, and perhaps even irreparable.

But while you may feel broken, I don't believe you actually are. Fragmented perhaps, the multiple parts of you bruised by the past you once occupied. And though those parts may still be hanging together, the fault lines have been left showing. Just like in an earthquake, every so often the tectonic plates of our lives shift, leaving the solid ground on which we once stood shaking and the lava seeping through. We are left clamoring to balance ourselves and make sense of the destruction and the altered landscape left behind.

That was the way it was for me when my husband died suddenly. With life upended, I spent the first two years after his death simply trying to regain a steady footing. It hasn't been an easy task to heal from the grief and loss that I've experienced, and it's something that I still live with every day. However, slowly, with time and the learnings you will find contained within the pages of this book, I've gently picked up the fragmented parts of myself and put them back together. Parts I didn't even realize were there until my world imploded. Thankfully, the bubbling lava of my traumatic loss has now subsided most days, and I have integrated his loss into the life I now live. Integration is a core goal of psychological work and involves building up your mind to enable yourself to navigate your emotions, understand your thoughts, and accept your reality, all while being in a relationship with yourself and others. I'd say that I'm at least some of the way there.

Over the years, many of my patients and clients have told me variations on the following theme: Though they know and understand something logically, they can often still feel differently to what their logic tells them is true. For example, I know logically that I shouldn't feel as guilty as I often do for being that friend who isn't particularly good at remembering birthdays, anniversaries, or replying to text messages in a timely way – but I still do feel guilty about it. I also know that I shouldn't feel responsible for other people's emotions, but somehow, sometimes, I still do. This reflects my underlying psychology.

There is, it would seem, a disparity between what we can acknowledge as logical and that which we feel. And how we feel is firstly driven by our thoughts. Wayne Dyer, an author and clinical psychologist whom I admire greatly, wrote a book called *Change Your Thoughts, Change Your Life*, which picks up this theme. And this also is where my book meets you, the reader. It's inherently human for your thoughts to reflect the negative or challenging things that have happened to you in your life. But letting those thoughts define you, and take over, can mean that you end up living a life not of your conscious choosing. My wish for you is to be able to choose a positive life consciously for yourself every single day. And how can you achieve this? By knowing yourself and your psychology inside out, and by being able to intervene effectively when things aren't going in the direction you want. In the chapters that follow, I'm going to help you to do just that.

Doing the Work to Heal

As a clinical psychologist, I've been trained within the British health system to assess, formulate, and treat all sorts of mental health problems and psychological disorders. My practice has been evidence-based and many of the people I've worked with have gotten better. However, I believe very strongly that my job through the years has merely been to facilitate my clients' own ability to heal. Through psychoeducation, building a trusting relationship with them, helping them to develop a new understanding of themselves and their circumstances, and providing them with the behaviors and strategies they need to thrive, the work I do increases my clients' own capacities for change and healing.

Often, we lack the knowledge and understanding we need about our mental health to make positive changes. Many of us also have a limited circle of trusted others who can, and will, encourage and authentically support us on our healing journey. And if the healing that we need is actually linked to our family dynamics and relationships, that makes it all the harder. All these factors and the wider stigma around mental health issues mean that we can end up suffering in silence, or worse, we may be actively discouraged from prioritizing our own mental health. This, in turn, means that we're denied the opportunity to develop new understanding and perspectives. Many of us have not been explicitly taught and modeled the skills we need to bolster and stabilize our own mental health and well-being. The therapeutic task, then, is for us to take responsibility for learning and teaching ourselves these things.

What I need you to know before you embark on the rest of this book is that I'm never the person who does the hard work in my clinical practice. That is down to my clients alone. I'm just the facilitator of the change. I would like you to view this book and what I hope to teach you in much the same way. It is the facilitator of the change you seek. And though this book and its contents can facilitate change, I cannot read it for you, nor do the work required. That will be down to you and the choices you make. And what an empowering choice it is: To know that we do have a say in how we approach our challenges.

Similarly, when my husband died, I had a choice to make about whether I stayed in bed and pulled the duvet over my head, or whether I was going to put two feet on the floor and keep moving forward. I feel fortunate that I had the knowledge, the support, and the encouraging network I needed to help me develop new perspectives and to be able to build the skills I needed to get through it. But I still had to show up every day and do the work. No matter how I felt, or what I'd experienced.

Trauma as a Guide

In many respects, this book is primarily a manifesto on trauma. It's about how all of us, in our own individual ways, are living with trauma as our companion. It's about normalizing the idea that trauma doesn't always stem from the big events, but involves the daily experiences that shape our personalities and how we relate to others. Throughout the book, you'll find stories of my own experiences and those of my clients, which I use to illustrate psychological concepts and ideas.

One such idea is that trauma has a way of changing who we are and how we respond. Trauma is not the 'event' that happened itself, but the ways in which our internal processes – thoughts, feelings, and behaviors – are forever changed in response to that event. I believe it is these internal changes that can leave us feeling as though we are broken. And this feeling of brokenness and fragmentation can also seem more acute depending on the nature of the traumatic event and how unexpected it was. And, crucially, I think most of us want to hide and suppress that fragmentation and pretend it's not there. But the truth is, all of us in our own ways are hiding the different parts of ourselves that feel broken or induce shame. Carl Jung called it the shadow self. Now we need to help you bring those parts of yourself out from the shadows and into the light, with the aim of helping you to feel whole again.

I believe that trauma isn't the life sentence that society purports it to be. In fact, it can teach us so much. My views are perhaps not as controversial as I sometimes fear they are, but I also know that there are those who won't agree with me. That's OK. I'm simply contributing to the conversation around mental health in a way that I hope is helpful to those of you who will align with what I have to say. And I hope that, in saying it, I can be both professional and relatable to you on your own journey.

A few years ago, I heard someone in the online space, I forget who, say the following words: 'Make your mess your message.' It resonated so deeply with me and I've worked toward this goal ever since. Like you, I'm a messy, complicated human. But I'm fortunate that in my mess, I've found my message. I'm sharing it now to help you make sense of your life – messy, complicated and nuanced as it will undoubtedly be.

How to Read This Book

The book is structured in three parts and offers exercises for you to complete as you read. This is intentional, as I want reading this book to be an active process of self-discovery.

If you wish, you can download a copy of the workbook with all the experiential exercises at the link **www.drlaurawilliams. com/whattodowhenbook**. I would also encourage you to start your own journal, in which you can write your reflections on the exercises.

In Part I, 'Meet Your Own Mind,' I introduce you to the importance of your unique story, developing your psychological mind (more on that later) and the ability to think in a psychologically informed way. In Chapter 1, I will invite you into the most vulnerable period of my life and how it led to my own psychological awakening, and the sort of realizations that I think many people arrive at following some important juncture or event in their life. I'll introduce you to the importance of the motivational hook that therapists and anyone doing psychological work must inevitably examine –

to find out the 'why' of the work. In Chapter 2, I share how psychological mindedness and mindfulness practices can help us to understand ourselves better. I also outline just how critical it is to slow everything down and really allow yourself to attune to your emotional experience, both in the here and now and when thinking about your past. In Chapter 3, we explore how trauma can actually have positive effects on us that are often forgotten about, and how these may offer you the chance to draw a line in the sand between who you have been in the past and who you are now, going forward.

Part II of the book, 'The Truth about Trauma,' delves more deeply into the psychological underpinnings of where trauma originates. In Chapter 4, I'll walk you through core concepts, including attachment and social modeling theory, and how we can apply these to ourselves. I also offer a broader definition of trauma and how it shows up in our relationships when we're growing up. In Chapter 5, we move on to talk about the cognitive monopoly on therapies, and how I believe CBT is not always the most helpful solution to what are often complex relational problems underlying the presenting problem. Reciprocity and what it means to good-quality relationships are also discussed.

In Chapter 6, we delve into the intergenerational nature of trauma and how our psychological well-being is influenced by biological, psychological, and social factors. We begin to examine how patterns of relating to others, known as schemas, reflect the different parts of ourselves and can influence our relational functioning with ourselves. In this chapter, I will also share a snapshot of the trauma patterns that have been passed down my personal family tree, from my grandmother to my mother, and then to me, to illustrate how intergenerational trauma can show up. Finally, I encourage you to develop your own trauma toolkit to manage the emotions that might arise while reading and working through the exercises in this book.

In the final part, 'The Tools to Heal,' I will familiarize you with what's required in any good psychological work. In Chapter 7, I outline just how pivotal psychological formulation is to understanding what it is that we then need to do about our circumstances – and, essentially, how that formulation informs the treatment. Simply put, a psychological formulation tells the story of how and why you may be struggling with a particular presenting problem such as, for example, depression, at a particular point in time. It offers a framework to consider the factors that influence the problem, making it better (protective factors) or worse (perpetuating factors). A formulation also draws links with past experiences. I also introduce you to my own four-step HEAL framework, which aligns roughly with the key components of good psychological work.

In Chapter 8, I offer an opportunity to consider one of the biggest barriers to psychological well-being: shame. I talk about cultivating compassion as an antidote to shame and how you might do that. In the final chapter, I offer suggestions for what you might actually need to do to cope with what you've been through. We'll explore the concept of powerfully imperfect living (with the problems of perfectionism forming an important strand throughout this book) and the Good Lives Model as a framework for gaining an even deeper understanding of how you want your life to look.

Self-Help as a Pathway to Change

Now, of course, reading a book and completing the work suggested in it isn't the same as receiving one-to-one therapy. But part of my rationale for writing this book is that I know all too well that access to good-quality, evidence-based therapy, and psychological information is difficult to come by these days. So, while reading this book doesn't constitute therapy, it does attempt to lift the veil on what therapy would ask of you and offers you the opportunity to do some of the work yourself.

However, this book is not the answer for you if you're in crisis. If you believe that you are, or need answers this book simply cannot provide, please seek appropriate support from a trained mental health professional in a timely way.

All said, I want you to know that self-help can be a powerful precursor to change. Many times over the years, I've seen how some people have struggled to move the needle far, even after months or years of psychological treatment. Then, seemingly out of nowhere, they make what looks like a spontaneous recovery. I've heard them say things like 'one day it all just clicked' and 'everything made sense.' But their recovery wasn't really spontaneous, of course. It was often preceded by months of work, growing understanding, and additional self-help on the side.

Recovery takes more than an hour's therapy once a week. It's a bit like those people who become 'overnight sensations' in a decade. Success is what happens when nobody is looking. And the work that leads to recovery is exactly the same. It takes commitment and effort, and sometimes it may feel like it's just not clicking – until one day it finally does. I feel passionate that the 'treatment' you need might not always be about individual therapy. It could be that this book is the beginning of your journey. Or perhaps you're using it as an add-on to the work you've already done, or are currently doing. Wherever you are and whatever you've done to reach this point, doing the work outlined in these pages will complement this.

Before you read on, here's one final thought for you to take with you on your journey: You are a product of all that's come before, and of all that's happened to you, both the good and the bad. You are an imperfect survivor and what has happened to you is not who you are. With adversity comes resilience, wisdom, and fortitude. I'm hopeful that you can pick up your 'broken parts' and put them back together to live a life as powerfully imperfect as you are.

Holding you in mind,

Laura
X

PART I

Meet Your Own Mind

CHAPTER 1

Awakening

He wakes with a start, jumping out of bed and asking me in panicked tones if I've heard the bang. It takes a moment for me to acclimatize to the space around us and understand what's happening. 'There was no bang,' I assure him. My words seem to make no sense, as he backs himself into the corner of our bedroom, wide-eyed.

Switching on the light and examining his fearful face, I can see that he isn't present in mind or body, and needs me to help him. To act now. Unfortunately, this isn't an unusual event for us. Matty, my husband of seven years, was diagnosed as a type 1 diabetic at the age of 24. Before this night, there've been at least three particularly notable occasions where he's experienced a hypoglycemic attack and an ambulance has been called to our house for assistance. Often, during these events, he can't think rationally and occasionally takes on a different persona to his usual laid-back self. Once, he had even had a seizure. Now, a single thought reverberates over and over in my mind, reassuring me. I've seen this before. And I know what I have to do.

As calmly as I can, I go downstairs to the kitchen to fetch some Lucozade, passing the bedrooms of my three children, all sound asleep. Lucozade is a sugary drink that should quickly rectify Matty's low sugar levels, if only I can coax him to drink it, which isn't always easy. As I return to the bedroom, I find him flopped onto his side of the bed, his muscles straining to hold up his slender 6ft 1in frame. I try to convince him to drink. He won't let me help him, but I know I need to keep trying.

The bright-orange drink spills and sloshes everywhere. Later, I will find the stains have seeped deep into the pale-blue walls of our bedroom. None left in the bottle, I make another urgent trip to the kitchen, scared to leave him alone again and realizing that I'm rapidly exhausting the possibility of pulling this situation back on my own.

When I return to the bedroom just a few seconds later, I'm shocked to find him lying prostrate across our bed. This is different now. He's desperately trying to grip the sides of the oak bedframe as a seizure takes hold. His fingers reach around the end of the bed, grappling for the sides. Somehow, I summon the strength to drag him onto the bedroom floor and place him in something resembling the recovery position.

Kneeling beside him as his body shakes, I call the ambulance. Then I call our families. Within minutes, both my family and his are here in the house with us. They live close by and can be with us quickly, and I need them here now, mostly to help with the children, as I do what I can for Matty before medical help arrives.

In the moments that followed, with his head cradled in my arms and supported by a pillow, his lips turn blue. He bites his tongue and bloody saliva leaks from his mouth onto the pillow. As I hold on to him, I realize how scared I feel. Silently waiting.

But even then, despite the horror unfolding, I believe that when help arrives, he'll be OK. I have seen this before.

As the medical team takes over, I go downstairs to check on my five-year-old daughter. She is now awake and sitting with my mum in the living room. I try to comfort her but don't want to linger. Running back upstairs, I meet my dad on the middle landing. As I catch his eye, he looks panicked and I can tell something's very wrong.

'What is it?' I implore. He's faltering for the words and opts for silence. 'What is it?' I scream this time.

Looking pained, he struggles to contain his emotions and the words 'He's not breathing,' splutter out of his mouth.

I immediately turn and fly up the remaining stairs, throwing myself across the threshold into our bedroom. By now, there are two crews of paramedics present. As my eyes dart back and forth over the scene, everyone looks to me as if they're too calm and not doing nearly enough. At first, I can't understand why.

My husband is lying in the space on the floor between our bed and the bathroom. His pajamas have been cut hastily from his body and there's medical equipment strewn across the carpet. Nobody looks me in the eye. I remember shouting, 'Can someone tell me what is going on?'

A male paramedic, standing to the side, lifts his head and says levelly, 'Matty isn't able to breathe for himself just now. We're going to ventilate him and take him to hospital.'

Frantically, I ask about his blood sugar. 'But this was just a hypo?' I say. A 'hypo' is a hypoglycemic attack when the blood sugar in the body is too low.

The man tells me Matty's blood sugar is high, not low. It's in this moment that I realize I don't understand what's happening. When this has happened before, his blood sugar was always low. My mind is racing as I try to make sense of it all – and fail.

I glance around the room and can finally see it in the faces of the medics. Then realization dawns: Matty isn't going to survive this. There is a calm resignation about how they're attending to him now and I can literally feel it. Nobody tells me; I just know. I can sense the lack of hope permeating what little air is left in the room. As they ventilate him, I slump to the ground and onto my hands and knees. I softly stroke Matty's feet and calves, willing the life to return to his body, begging him silently through my tears not to leave us. But I know the medics are simply buying time.

Minutes later, I go back downstairs, past the bedroom where my two-year-old twin boys were sleeping soundly just minutes before. My dad is in there playing with them, shielding them from the horror of what's unfolding. In the living room, my mum is still with my daughter. I go in again to check on her. She tells me, 'Everything will be OK, Mummy.' She, too, believes she has seen this before and is calm in the predictability of it. Daddy sometimes gets unwell. The ambulance comes and then he gets better. Simple.

I can't look her in the eye as I pull her close. Here, in the living room, the noise of the life support machine pumping hard on his chest in the bedroom directly overhead is deafening. It feels like it's shaking the foundations of our home. Shaking the foundations of our world.

Finally, the paramedics are ready to move him. I'm not allowed to travel in the ambulance and I don't protest. I get dressed to follow separately. As I stand waiting in the hallway while they bring him downstairs and take him out of the front door, an older female medic descends the staircase. She glances at my tear-stained face and says simply, 'What has happened here?' to no one in particular. Somehow, her words make me feel guilty. Like I'm responsible. Nobody answers. As I leave, my mum attempts to say something comforting. I look back at her and say, 'He's going to die, Mum.' I can tell she doesn't believe me, but I feel certain of it.

In the resuscitation suite at our local hospital, I hold Matty's hand tight in mine, periodically placing my forehead to his chest, letting my tears fall unhindered onto his pale skin. I whisper quietly into his ear that I will always love him. That I will ensure our children will know of him and that he will be forever present in their lives. As the minutes tick past, his breathing changes. It becomes shallower. Labored. I don't want him to leave us behind. And then, too quickly, his last breath comes and goes. He is quiet now. It is 3.42 a.m. when a doctor calls the time of death.

As my head falls to rest again on Matty's bare chest, I finally let out the full force of my anguish. I can feel my heart, heavy inside my chest. I ask myself, *How can this heart of mine be pumping life-force through me while his has now stopped forever?* I miss his good heart already.

Eventually, I let go of his hand and sit down on a chair at the side of the bed. It feels too far away. I move it closer. I watch his family say their goodbyes, immeasurable pain etched on their faces. We are, all of us, stunned. I look at his face, still stained with bloody saliva, and have the urge to wash him. I ask a nurse if I can. She tells me that they will wash his body and then we can sit with him in a different room; for now, we have to leave this place. I don't know if this sort of thing simply isn't allowed. I nod and sit back. I wanted to do this so badly – as one of the last acts of kindness and intimacy as his wife – but I don't have the strength to fight for it in this moment. That I never got to fulfil my wish will be a regret I hold forever.

We are ushered into another room, and I don't know it but this will be the last time I touch him. We seem to spend far too short a time with him, before someone suggests we should leave. I let go of Matty's hand for the last time and turn to walk from the room. I can't remember how far I get before my legs and my head tell me to stop. I break down and the urge to go back and stay longer with him surfaces. His mum puts her arm around my back and physically guides me to keep moving. And so I do. The world is quiet and still outside as we slump into the car and begin the silent drive home.

Life Lessons

There is nothing like experiencing the sudden and untimely death of the person you love to shatter any illusion you may have held of a 'perfect' or charmed life. It comes seemingly out of nowhere, turning your reality upside down. Just a month before my husband's death, we had been sitting in the waiting area of a smart Edinburgh clinic about to have the medicals that were the last step in obtaining visas to go to live and work in Australia. This was a dream that Matty and I had shared since meeting in our early twenties. We talked of it at length over the years and even went on honeymoon to Australia to sample the lifestyle there for ourselves. We hoped that it'd be an adventure, offer work opportunities for us both, and a way of living that would suit our family. Ironically, that day we were both given a clean bill of health and our visas were rubber-stamped. Four weeks later, Matty was dead and the dream of what our life could have been was shattered.

Now let me be clear. It's not that we had a completely 'perfect' life. But I had known and felt that we were very lucky to have the life we did have. We had great family and friends around us, jobs that supported our lifestyle, and three healthy children. We could afford to go on holidays, and we were happy. It was 'perfect' to us. But increasingly, I had harbored thoughts that perhaps we couldn't be this lucky. Could we? That something would be coming down the line for us one day.

If you think about it logically, I guess that's true for most of us.

> At some point, all of us will experience
> the loss of someone we love, and face a
> health issue or some other life crisis.

But I never imagined that I would be left living life without the partner I had chosen just a few short years beforehand. In her book *Daring Greatly*, the American author Brené Brown has termed this type of thinking as 'foreboding joy': a feeling of contentment or happiness, followed immediately by the worry of what might come along to erase it.

And what did I do when life as I knew it was taken from me? Well, I did what I knew how to do. I started coping. I was very good at knowing what had to be done, and getting on and doing it. I plastered on a brave face and started working through the necessities of living with three small children. Daily, I tackled the admin of death. And I didn't just work through it. I excelled at it. I was a high achiever and this was another thing I knew I could work through, step by step, until I met my goal.

I didn't comprehend then that there would be no endpoint. No goal to reach. That his death would be a constant forever. But at that time, I was simply in survival mode and reverting to the well-worn patterns for how I'd coped in my 35 years of life up to that point. This was expressed in so many ways. That first night after Matty died, I remember my mum gently suggesting that she would stay with me in the house overnight. I refused point-blank. I had a strong feeling that I'd need to start as I meant to go on and I'd always been fiercely independent. I was now on my own and that was how it was going to be. Plain and simple.

Back then, I didn't see it for what it was.

I was pushing people away from my pain.

I didn't feel comfortable letting anyone witness the sheer agony of my grief. What I learned later was that others witnessing my loss would eventually become a comfort. But in those early days, I couldn't allow myself to be fully supported. I believed that if I could just manage to control it all, then everything would be OK… The trademark moves of a classic perfectionist, trying to regain control of an altogether uncontrollable situation.

Adjusting to Each Moment

Around three days after Matty died, the kids asked me to get the paddling pool out. It was July. The school holidays had begun and the weather was unusually hot for Scotland. So, there

I was – in a swimming costume, in my back garden, blowing up a paddling pool, and desperately trying to make life appear and feel normal for the kids. I remember feeling faint as I breathed air into that paddling pool, one breath after another until it was done. And though I breathed, the heart that pumped oxygen through me was broken.

The realization that my children would never know their dad fully was overwhelming. That he would never walk my daughter, Ella, down the aisle on her wedding day. This thought still makes me weep today. I often wonder whether, if the day comes, she will ask me to 'give her away' in his absence. Will she get married at all?

From the moment Matty drew his last breath, I instinctually ascribed to the notion that it was my job to make all of this 'OK' for my children. That I had to ameliorate their pain and heartache somehow. It was all down to me now. My responsibility. These days, I know that I'm not responsible for ridding my children of their pain. Their pain is the displaced love they feel for their dad. However, I am responsible for sitting with them as they experience it, and teaching them that it won't always feel as it does in their most difficult moments.

Of course, because of the initial pressure I put on myself, there were moments where I unraveled. These were often experienced privately, after dark with the curtains drawn and the kids safely tucked up in bed. Sometimes, I would use red wine to numb my feelings. Sometimes, I used wine to access them. It didn't matter which, because at this stage, my grief wasn't being witnessed fully and I certainly wasn't processing my emotions in any meaningful way.

However, looking back, I was quick off the mark to give myself the sort of things that I might suggest to a client going through a loss like mine. I joined a support group for people who'd been widowed young, and I attended coffee meets and events with the kids. I joined a triathlon club to move my body. I also organized a couple of appointments with a private psychologist and with an old mentor of mine from clinical training, who had himself lost a spouse early. On the face of it, these all looked like healthy and adaptive strategies. However, if I'm honest with myself now, I viewed these things like a checklist in my mind. The perfectionism I'd relied on for years had come to the fore. I was in a pattern of action and striving – rather than allowing myself the emotional space to be vulnerable, to heal. That came much later.

Putting It in Writing

At some point, I began writing. Initially, this was to help me remember things through the mind-fog of my grief. I wanted to have a reliable testimony that I could use one day as an aide-mémoire to talk to my children about what had happened.

However, in writing my experiences down, I found both my voice and the multitude of emotions that all those perfectionistic actions and that striving of mine had been suppressing. My feelings poured onto the page alongside my tears.

> Through writing, I could access my grief,
> and it cracked me open from the inside out.

Tentatively, I began to share my writing in the form of blogs and posts on social media. These resonated with people and eventually the blogs became a journal and writing prompts, and later a self-published book, *Grief Writer: A Journal*. This helped both build my own path toward healing and create a legacy of Matty's life that would help others on their journeys through processing the emotions of loss.

First and foremost, writing became a safe space that I could escape to. And at that time, I wanted to escape everything. The reality of his death. The endless yet well-meaning messages that lit up my phone at all hours of the day and night. The smell of my home filled with so many lilies it reeked of death.

I also wanted to escape the people. So many people. The police officers I had to speak to, because of the sudden nature of his death. The visitors who would pop by to check in. The parents who blindsided me in the playground when my daughter returned to school, with questions like, 'How are you?', 'How are the kids?' or worse still, 'So, what actually happened?' How do you even begin to answer questions like this, especially when they were asked by people who were often near strangers?

Once, I was even introduced to someone as having lost my husband just weeks before. This woman looked at me pityingly as she said in her broad West Lothian accent, 'Och hen – I know how ye feel. When I lost my husband a couple of years ago, I was devastated.' This woman was likely in her seventies. Outwardly, I smiled and nodded. Internally, I was screaming that I was 35 with three kids and my husband didn't make his 38th birthday. She did not know how I felt.

What I realized, as I became more and more enraged by these relational exchanges, was just how sickeningly agreeable I was all the time.

I would deny my true feelings
to avoid any awkwardness and to
ensure nobody else felt bad.

I pushed how I felt so far down into the pit of my stomach that many people might not have known there was anything wrong with me at all – far less that I'd been widowed only a few short weeks beforehand. And I felt responsible for everything.

So there I was. A 35-year-old widow. A clinical psychologist who worked with people to help them uncover and validate their own emotions and childhood experiences. Yet, unbelievably, this was when the real learning about my own psychological make-up began. I was finally taking ownership of how often I took to suppressing my emotional experiences in order to be liked. No, more than that – *approved of.* Believe me when I tell you that this is still a work in progress.

My Own Psychology

I was first introduced to the academic concept of perfectionism in 2004, when completing my undergraduate dissertation at the University of Stirling, Scotland. My supervisor for the project was Professor Rory O'Connor, a world-renowned expert on suicide. He was an incredibly smart, dynamic, and engaging lecturer, and – as I later discovered – a kind and patient teacher.

After lectures with him, I always felt so enthusiastic about psychological research and how it applied to real life. I knew I wanted him to supervise my final-year project, but I was keen to approach him with an established plan. I put some time and effort into thinking this through and resolved that when I did approach him, it would be with a final-year project that would be difficult to refuse. I needed to bide my time and put in the groundwork first.

Meanwhile, I'd heard about a career module I could take as an additional course for extra credits alongside my degree. It looked interesting as it meant interviewing someone who was doing an applied job in the field of psychology. I was always looking to explore where my degree might take me in the real world, so I joined the module.

While on the module, I met a fellow student who was in the same year as me and studying psychology, too. We got on well and agreed that, as we were both interested in the same things, we should jointly interview an honorary lecturer within the department who was also an applied psychologist. Professor Kevin Power had worked in Scottish prisons – and that was the role we wanted to interview him about. After emailing our request and making an appointment with him in advance, off we went with our notebooks and carefully prepared questions to fulfil the module's requirements.

As predicted, Professor Power gave us a fascinating insight into the types of work a psychologist could do in forensic settings. That day, he told us that work within the Scottish Prison Service would be 'the best apprenticeship' we would ever get. His words made a lasting impression on me and working for the Scottish Prison Service became my new goal.

I'd always been fascinated by extreme criminal behavior and now I was being told there was a great route into the sort of job that I wanted. My perfectionistic brain went into overdrive. There was about a year to go until I was due to graduate, and

I knew I needed to get some real-world experience that would put me in the best possible place to gain a graduate position. I began doing nursing shifts at a local hospital, while constantly scanning for any roles that might take me closer to my dream job.

A few months later, and living in a new flat with the same student I'd met on my career module, no less, I was ecstatic when I saw a job advertised for a summer student position within Her Majesty's Prison and Young Offenders Institute at Polmont. I excitedly told my roommate about it and applied. It meant a summer job and hard-to-come-by experience that would bring me closer to my goal.

The day of my interview, my roommate offered to drive me to the prison. After arriving at the reception, I was asked to sign the registration sheet and provide some identification. As the prison officer at the gate slid the sheet across the desk to me, one name stood out. There, on the sign-in sheet directly below my name, was my roommate's name. In disbelief, I signed the form and handed it back, wondering why she had applied and chosen not to tell me.

Admittedly, I felt more than a little betrayed. However, I tell you this story to illustrate how all I could think about in that moment was how that job had to be mine. I wasn't even particularly focused on any perceived deception on the part of my roommate. I was resolved to land the position. Why? Because failure simply wasn't an option for me.

Now, I got the job. But what if I hadn't? How would it have felt to have been met with a no? How would I have reacted had my roommate got the job instead of me? Retrospectively, I would imagine that younger, naive version of me would have felt crushed. Humiliated, even. Because anything less than me walking away with an offer of employment wouldn't have been good enough. My perfectionism and fear of failure – though I didn't recognize it as such at the time – sometimes came with the benefit of improving my performance. But that wouldn't always be the case.

A few weeks after my offer of employment for the summer at HMPYOI Polmont, I stood outside Professor Rory O'Connor's office and knocked on the door. I was ready to pitch a final-year dissertation project that involved interviewing young offenders in a real-life Scottish jail. I was hopeful and ready. As I'd hoped, he agreed to tutor me, and so began my introduction to psychological research and the role of perfectionism in mental health. What I learned that summer would stay with me long after I handed my set of jail keys back. However, what I hadn't anticipated was that I would also be learning about myself and who I was underneath all my own childhood conditioning. (Conditioning means the ways in which our thoughts, feelings, and behaviors have been shaped by our relational experience with others such as caregivers.)

The Price of Perfectionism

Perfectionism is one of those terms that gets thrown around too much for my liking. In recent years, it's become a popular way of describing people who strive to achieve and do their best, in a broadly similar way to how obsessive compulsive disorder (OCD) is now spoken of. Too often, I hear statements like, 'Oh, she's such a perfectionist,' or, 'You know how I like things to be exactly right, I'm a bit OCD.' Incidentally, psychological research has long noted the relatedness of perfectionism and obsessive compulsive disorder (Frost and Steketee, 2007). But the point I want to make is that speaking about perfectionism in this way diminishes the very real suffering it can cause individuals. Perfectionism has been linked to many psychological disorders, but for many people like me, it shows up in what may at first seem like relatively benign ways.

When asked about perfectionism, most people will tell you it's when we strive to do things 'just right' or correctly; that it's about making sure whatever we do is done to the very best of our ability. And if this is perfectionism, it doesn't sound that terrible, does it? Often, it isn't. Perfectionism, as far as psychological traits go, can be helpful, up to a point. In fact, early research previously categorized perfectionism as either positive and healthy, or negative and pathological (Hamachek, 1978). It can allow us to meet the standards set for us and sometimes even exceed them. This can have a positive impact on our scholastic record, our career, and even what people think of us.

And therein lies one of the first challenges of perfectionism and many other psychological traits: It's something that we're often praised for. As children, when we do things 'right,' this behavior is frequently positively reinforced by those around us. When we defer to authority and minimize our own needs, our parents, teachers, mentors, and sports coaches – to name a few – may view this as 'good behavior' and tell us so. We feel validated by the praise and then strive for more of it, because the emotional experience of it is so pleasurable. Before we know it, we're demanding and expecting perfection from ourselves to replicate that emotional pleasure and the dopamine hit that being praised offers us. And that's before we've even thought about the other key underlying mechanism through which perfectionism can arise: social modeling (*see page 72*).

In a 2015 paper on the topic, Professor Joachim Stoeber described perfectionism as 'a personality disposition characterized by striving for flawlessness and setting exceedingly high standards of performance accompanied by overly critical evaluations of one's behaviour' (Stoeber, 2015, p.171). Stoeber was summarizing perfectionism research over a number of decades. But despite how well-known the concept of perfectionism is, its component parts are less so. There are three main types of perfectionism. Hewitt and Flett (1991) outlined these as:

1. Self-oriented perfectionism

2. Other-oriented perfectionism

3. Socially-prescribed perfectionism

Self-oriented perfectionism is most well-known of the trio and what most people would describe if you asked them about perfectionism. This type of perfectionism is when we hold ourselves to high standards and can be self-critical if we fall short. Other-oriented perfectionism is when we expect those around us – our family, friends, or colleagues – to perform to a high standard and do things as we would do them. Socially-prescribed perfectionism is when we believe those around us – family, friends, and colleagues – expect perfectionism of us.

It's important to be aware of all three types of perfectionism to understand this personality trait within yourself. This is something many of my therapy clients struggle with, and which I think is more common than we may realize. To help shape your own thinking on this, let me share with you one woman's narrative of perfectionism. As you read it, ask yourself whether you can relate to any of the details.

A VICIOUS CIRCLE OF PERFECTION

This is the story of a woman who holds high expectations of both herself and others. At work, she struggles to delegate tasks to her colleagues, as she believes she will do a better job. She likes the feeling of being in control. That way, nothing can go wrong.

But this means that she has a tendency to take on too much and she can struggle to keep up as a result. This can lead to making simple mistakes, which she then overly berates herself for. This, in turn, triggers her underlying core belief of not being good enough and means she procrastinates further and occasionally misses deadlines – a self-fulfilling prophecy.

At home, she sometimes feels resentful that her partner never seems to do as much as she does around the house. But when he does attempt to help her, she can often be critical of his efforts, which can give rise to some tension. On other days, her reaction can be quite different and when she sees him starting a household task, she will apologize, as she can feel like these should be her sole responsibility and that her partner believes this, too.

Her high expectations can sometimes extend to her children. She holds certain ideas about what they 'should' be able to do for themselves and can become frustrated, believing they are deliberately choosing not to do what she asks of them. She has stepchildren and often struggles with the idea that they think she isn't 'motherly enough' or, worse still, that she is the stereotypical evil stepmother.

She has a higher-than-average level of self-awareness around her perfectionism and other relational patterns. However, that doesn't always mean it's easy to catch herself and change her behavior.

In the example just given, all three types of perfectionism are in existence. However, the one that fascinates me most is socially-prescribed perfectionism. This is where she believes that her partner expects perfectionism from her around the house. He doesn't, by the way.

How do I know this? Well, because that woman is me. Bet you weren't expecting that, were you? Perfectionism is one of the 'flavors' of my own psychological dysfunction and something that I recognize as having been problematic for me for years. It has developed in response to my fear of failure and is partly to do with the competitive environments I've been exposed to – sport and the profession of psychology among them. I also have a tendency toward minimizing my needs in favor of those of others' and taking responsibility for other people's feelings. Another of the many impacts of my own childhood conditioning.

Now, just in case my mum or dad is reading this, or if you yourself are questioning the validity of 'blaming' our current behaviors on our childhoods and by extension our parents or other primary caregivers, I want to say something important here. I'm not in the business of externalizing blame. I am in the business of taking responsibility. And not the kind of responsibility where I take ownership of things that are not mine to take responsibility for.

Let me explain further. My psychological challenges exist because some of this behavior was modeled to me, sure. My mum had high expectations placed on her, too, by her own parents, and, in this way, we can see the intergenerational nature of our psychological makeup (*we'll look at this in more detail in Chapter 6*). But these behaviors of perfectionism and subjugating my own needs developed in a home that was also loving and supportive, and where other incredibly positive, adaptive, and helpful behaviors were modeled, too. I know this won't be the case for everyone, but often our parents are simply doing the best they know how, with the resources, knowledge, and energy they have at the time. I'm a parent, too, and I often do things with all the best intentions and still don't get it right all the time.

But here's something you should know:

> The ruptures that happen in our
> relationships are never as important as
> the way that we choose to repair them.

I have chosen to repair my ways of relating to myself and others by questioning the behavioral strategies that once served me, but no longer do so. My mum and dad aren't 'to blame.' They are part of me and my story. Just as their parents were part of them and theirs. And to change any of it, we need to take ownership and become fully responsible for what happens next. The author and motivational speaker Mel Robbins says it best when she tells us, 'There is no one else coming to save you.' And the good news is, you can do that all by yourself. I believe, with the right knowledge and attitude, you can heal from the shadows of unhelpful childhood conditioning.

After waking up to my own perfectionistic tendencies and my avoidance of emotions or saying how I truly felt after my husband died, I decided to take ownership of my individual psychology. I now view myself as a recovering perfectionist and am quick to identify this trait when it arises. I'm learning to release control and to delegate tasks in my work and at home. This approach is also allowing me the opportunity to demonstrate better leadership and more conscious parenting. I'm more mindful of my workload and can rest when I need to without that inner self-criticism rearing its head. My confidence has been boosted by the imperfect action I take, and this has helped confirm my reframed core belief that 'I am enough.'

I'm still working on understanding how and why these core beliefs developed in the first place. I can see how the expectations placed on me by myself and others when I was growing up have shaped my life.

> I am a work in progress, but can
> now see myself more clearly.

I am cultivating compassion for the vulnerable child within me that was used to well-worn patterns of relating to others. Sometimes, she comes to visit me and I welcome her with open arms, asking her, 'What do you need today?' At home, my current partner and I now operate more as a team. I communicate my needs better and have let some things go, in the knowledge that they aren't as important as I might once have believed. Finally, I realize the expectations I sometimes hold for my kids are not always age-appropriate. And with tasks that are, I'm becoming more patient in scaffolding their learning around them. Life feels very different now that I am embracing imperfection and trusting that all will be OK. And I know that this can be your experience, too, when you examine your own conditioning fully and build your awareness of what needs to change.

Given all I've just shared with you, I want you to imagine that a different reality is possible for you, too. A reality in which you understand fully how your developmental history has shaped your individual psychology and the person you have become – both the adaptive aspects of yourself and the unhelpful ones. I can also tell you that change and personal growth are possible, and I'm here to show you how, step by step.

And, of course, perfectionism is just one psychological trait that's part of my story. There are countless expressions of our individual psychological makeup. I want to help you become aware of yours, whatever they are. My awakening came over many years, with the final catalyst being my husband's untimely death. You may be at the very start of your journey and you don't need to wait on a traumatic loss or life event to begin the work of inner change.

> Wherever you are, I want to hold you by
> the hand as we journey together toward
> your own psychological awakening.

'You Gotta Roll with It'

As this first chapter concludes, I want you to start this work today with an exercise to examine your motivation. In schema therapy (*more on that later*), we often talk about the motivational hook – the reason why we want to engage in inner work – and it's a key component to consider when embarking on therapeutic self-development.

The following exercise will encourage you to understand why it is that you want to do this work. Is it because you're in a cycle of anxiety or depression that you can't seem to get out of? Is it because you wish to consider how your own psychology is impacting your parenting, relationships, or work life? Perhaps doing this work is the ultimate act of self-care that has been lacking in your life? Or could it be that having a deeper understanding of yourself might remove the limitations that have plagued your belief of what is possible for you? Whatever your 'why,' think of doing this and all the other exercises in this book as part of your commitment to yourself – that you are finally starting a worthwhile journey from which there's no turning back.

I wonder if that sounds scary to you? I once had a patient who, after just a few sessions, seemed particularly aggrieved when he arrived one day. When we explored the issue, he acknowledged his anger. He told me he'd gained new perspective. He was no longer able to hide behind the defended narrative he had created around a traumatic life event years earlier. He was finally seeing it for what it was, what it meant, and how he had attempted to cope with it across his life. His anger was a response to his knowing that he would never now be able to unsee this new narrative.

Self-development work is powerful and you must be ready. Only you will know if you are.

Now, with all that said, I firmly believe that motivation is one of the biggest lies we have ever been told. Working with people closely over the last 20 years in clinical practice has taught me that people aren't typically motivated to change their behavior. Discipline is hard. And the other thing about doing this work is that it brings up resistance – which you need to prepare for. It is a normal and expected part of the process and doesn't mean you should give up. Resistance is what happens when we are being asked to change, and our response is to deny or minimize our problems and our personal responsibility for them. Some of the resistance behaviors we might notice include perfectionism, criticizing the therapist or therapeutic modality, being self-critical, and wanting to be seen as independent and invulnerable. Not surprisingly, shame lies at the heart of why resistance comes up for people (Teyber and Teyber, 2010).

One of my husband's favorite bands was a group called Oasis. He knew practically every lyric of every song by heart. And in one famous Oasis song there's a message I need you to hear before you read any further: The message is that you've got to roll with it. What am I talking about in this instance? Resistance.

'Rolling with resistance' is a common phrase used by therapists in psychological work. The term was originally coined by the clinical psychologists Miller and Rollnick, who used a motivational interviewing approach to help people who were attempting to stop smoking (Miller and Rollnick, 1991).

It is natural and only to be expected that when you are trying to do something differently, some resistance will arise.

Some of you may be at the pre-contemplative stage and have never considered that building psychological awareness was something you'd ever need to do. Others may be ambivalent about doing psychological work and making changes; for example, you might hold powerful reasons to do this work and make changes, and equally powerful reasons not to. Wherever you are on your journey, my hope is that this book will act as your companion along the way. Let's take the first step now, and reflect on your reasons and readiness to do the psychological work that will help to take you from a place of feeling broken to the possibility of a brighter future.

MOTIVATIONAL EXERCISE

Here are some questions to consider before you move on to Chapter 2. Take some time to reflect, and in your journal write down your answers to the following motivation exercise.

1. What is your immediate reaction to the ideas presented in this chapter? What are your predominant thoughts and feelings?

2. Are there any areas of obvious resistance for you?

3. What function do you think these areas of resistance serve for you?

4. If you're keen to understand your own psychology, what is your motivation to do so?

5. What's held you back from psychological work or understanding before now?

6. What have you realized about your own psychological story already, simply from having started the process of placing conscious attention on it?

CHAPTER 2

Getting to Know Yourself

The concept of psychological mindedness is highly relevant in the field of psychology, but, in my view, rarely receives the attention it deserves. It's one of the first things I consider when deciding whether to take someone on for therapy. Why? Well, the more psychologically minded you are, the more likely you will be able to engage in the therapeutic process and make lasting changes. However, if you first need to build your psychological mindedness (known as PM), this can affect how long the therapeutic process takes and how successful it may be.

Like most things in life, our level of psychological mindedness exists on a spectrum. Researchers have found that those people with a high degree of psychological mindedness – high-PM people – understand that psychological constructs are fundamental to our overall functioning and psychological well-being. Yet very few of us today have likely ever considered just how psychologically minded we are or how this might be impacting our satisfaction in life. That's why I'm going to outline in this chapter what psychological mindedness is, why it's critical to our happiness, and how it can be cultivated.

Psychological mindedness has been defined as 'a degree of access to one's feelings that leads, through discussion of one's own problems with others, to an ability to acquire insight into the meaning and motivation of one's own and others' thoughts, feelings, and behaviour, and to a capacity for change' (Conte and Ratto, 1997, p.21). So psychological mindedness isn't only about the self and our understanding of why we think and feel the way we do, but our ability to understand others.

The ability to understand other people's motivations and feelings is also known as 'perspective-taking.' That is, being able to put yourself into another person's shoes to explore things from their point of view. It makes sense, I think, that the ability to perspective-take is adaptive and helpful to us as human beings. It allows us to function more successfully in our relationships, as we seek to understand others and perhaps change how we relate to them as a consequence.

I cannot overstate the importance of understanding the self and others as a mechanism to reflect on both your past and present experiences in relationships.

If, for example, your psychological mindedness is low, then this leaves you in the dark, grappling to understand the motivations of others and perhaps reaching conclusions about your experiences in relation to them that may exacerbate your own psychological pain. The meaning we take from things matters, and when our psychological mindedness is low, there's a chance that the narrative we're formulating in our mind about our past experiences and relationships is flawed or even false.

Now, I should also say here that perspective-taking is something that neurodivergent individuals are likely to struggle with more than others. The impaired 'theory of mind' – the ability to understand other people by attributing mental states to them – that exists in individuals with ADHD and autism, for example, has also been found to be present in people with certain psychological disorders such as anorexia nervosa (Bora et al., 2016). This can mean that it's more challenging for these people to understand the perspective of others fully. So it's worth being aware of this if you yourself are neurodivergent or perhaps currently struggling psychologically, as this can inevitably have an impact on your ability to think psychologically.

As a psychologist, I'm going to say I'm usually pretty good at understanding my own thoughts and feelings, and those of others. It's literally my job to reflect on them. But I also know that I have a tendency toward not giving my emotions the space they deserve. I wonder how many of you reading this will recognize that pattern in yourself...

In my case, I know that leading a very full life means I often believe I don't have enough time to dedicate to self-reflection and emotional processing. However, this can also be driven by an avoidance of vulnerability and how uncomfortable we can feel sitting with our emotions.

> I want to help empower more people
> like you to think psychologically
> about themselves.

Developing psychological mindedness and understanding is an important life skill and one that cannot be overlooked when you're on a self-development journey.

Mindedness and Mindfulness

No exploration of psychological mindedness would be complete without considering the concept of mindfulness. Mindfulness is 'the state of being attentive to and aware of what is taking place in the present' (Brown and Ryan, 2003, p.822). In recent years, there has been an explosion of 'mindfulness' into the psychological space, as third-wave therapies have been explored, researched, and adopted by mainstream psychology to augment traditional cognitive behavioral therapies and techniques. Third-wave therapies often utilize concepts such as acceptance, spirituality, and, of course, mindfulness, which have arisen from Eastern traditions, as opposed to traditional Western ideologies.

Mindfulness was originally utilized within an eight-week therapeutic program aimed at stress reduction (Kabat-Zinn, 1979). In many ways, it's become fashionable to say that we practice mindfulness, but I'm not always confident that people understand why it can be so important for our psychological health. Mindfulness offers us an opportunity for what schema therapy would call attunement. Attunement is that ability to be present with, acknowledge, recognize, and really feel our feelings. Attunement is the opposite of the avoidance of emotions that I mentioned earlier. And, though it has a fancy name, attunement doesn't have to be a fancy process. It could even mean dedicating just a few short minutes to getting curious about what your emotional experience is in the moment. At the end of this chapter, I'll be asking you to develop your own attunement practice to support you in this work – one that works for you. But before that, I'd like to tell you about my first experience of mindfulness.

After completing my undergraduate degree in psychology, my first job in the NHS was working within an intensive eating disorder team that helped very low-weight patients struggling with anorexia nervosa. In my role as an assistant psychologist, I was offered various learning opportunities. It was here that I was introduced to mindfulness and mindfulness-based techniques. Each week, I was invited to take part in a mindfulness class. The group was made up of a mixture of clinicians, therapists, and caregivers of patients with eating disorders. Gathering in a large, high-ceilinged room, the more seasoned mindfulness practitioners would arrive with yoga mats and blankets, and set themselves up on the floor. Shoes off, socks poking out the end of cozy blankets.

I had a visceral reaction to attending this group. Discomfort! I remember being curious about how these (some quite senior) clinicians seemed unfazed by lying around on the floor, eyes closed, and vulnerable for all to see. It felt somehow unprofessional to me. I opted to sit in a high-backed leather chair. I had no blanket and struggled to keep my eyes shut, instead opening one eye tentatively to peek across the room. I can still smell the warm mustiness of that space with the sun streaming through the tall bay window. I struggled to sit still. Out of nowhere, I would feel an itch and be compelled to scratch it, and the spell of my 'mindful' focus would be broken.

Of course, many people approach mindfulness that way – with a sense that it must be perfect. I know I did, and it simply didn't work… I couldn't lean into the vulnerability of it. At the time, rather than recognize that the problem lay with me and the fact that I was learning a new skill, I externalized the issue, choosing instead to believe that it was mindfulness itself that was the problem. I labeled it as a bit 'woo-woo' and nothing to do with psychotherapy or true psychological understanding.

Today, many years later, I know different. Mindfulness is one of the key components to knowing your own psychology in the here and now. It invites you to step away from the external world, sit with yourself, even if only for a minute, and truly examine your current internal emotional state. Without mindful attunement in the present moment, how can we then loop back and understand how our emotional functioning today might have been set by our past experiences? And, to be clear, mindfulness is not prescriptive. It doesn't necessarily mean attending a group practice. It doesn't have to mean yoga mats, soft blankets, and closed eyes. It simply means taking the time to sit with and explore your true feelings. Whichever way you choose to do that is entirely up to you. But make no mistake, mindfulness is important. Lastly, mindfulness does not always equate to meditation, though there are often, of course, mindful elements within meditation too.

The last thing I will say about this is that there's a general rule of thumb I use when considering my emotional state and that of my clients. It's this: If I'm overthinking and ruminating about my past, then I make it more likely that my mood will be impacted and I will experience feelings of sadness or depression. If I'm worrying and obsessing about my future, then I make it more likely that I will feel anxious and overwhelmed. Mindfulness asks us to step out of past and future thinking, and just be in the present. In this way we find contentment.

Mindfulness, to me, is a way of
protecting your peace.

Past Meeting Present

There's a common cliché about going to see a psychologist, therapist, or 'shrink' – that they'll sit you down and say, 'So, can you tell me about your childhood?' This notion of what psychological work is has become so common that it's now an easy way to ridicule the profession. But why isn't our childhood a valid place to start? Our history must inform our future and I believe with my whole heart that we heal through telling our stories. And to tell our whole story we must start at the beginning.

I do believe that part of the criticism that's levelled at my profession around this issue is again to do with avoidance. If your childhood has been challenging in some way, it's of course natural that you don't necessarily want to revisit it. After all, it's a self-protective mechanism to rubbish something we feel fearful of. Talking about events can also be experienced as reliving them. And in truth, nobody really wants to relive the most traumatic experiences of their lives. But there can be value in doing so.

When you examine more fully the meaning you have gleaned from past events, you can reframe them, if appropriate to do so, and give yourself the space to process the emotions that arise as a result. Writing the first section of this book, in which I recounted the circumstances of the night my husband died, was difficult for this very reason. It's hard to put yourself back into events that have an emotional temperature to them. But, as I've said previously, writing has allowed me to process what happened over and over again, deriving new meaning with time. I can now read that section of the book without the tears flowing as they once did. It's not that I care less; it's because the emotional temperature has reduced through repeated exposure to what happened in a way that has felt safe.

I often have clients who, in my first sit-down with them, will say something like, 'I need help with my mood, but I don't need or want to talk about my childhood.' Some are more fervent in their view than others, but it gives me an initial impression of where they are in their openness toward vulnerability. I gently explain why I must understand their backstory, and how the stories of their lives and their experiences shape them. Some don't want to continue. Some do.

I can say with certainty that our childhood is important and my goal as a therapist is to help you understand where past meets present. Imagine you come to my consulting room struggling with anxiety. It limits you in your daily life. You overthink decisions and often cancel plans you've made with friends, because you just can't face it. And when you cancel the plans, you get immediate relief from those anxious feelings. Nonetheless, you want this cycle to be different, as you know that when you do go out and socialize you'll feel the better for it. This might describe many people reading this book. But you are, all of you, unique. This is why I need to know your whole story. I need to capture the uniqueness of each individual in any psychological assessment I undertake.

The same behavior might have very different functions and meet different individual needs, depending on the person. Let's say that when we delve a bit deeper into your childhood, it becomes clear that anxiety was a behavior modeled to you by your dad. Each and every time you were preparing to leave the house, he became very stressed and shouty. You became anxious in response. You learned that going out was a time of peak stress and worry. Your emotional experience was never acknowledged or validated.

Through the process of a holistic psychological assessment, it becomes evident that you often felt like you were walking on eggshells around your dad – not just when trying to leave the house. Consequently, you became hypervigilant to his emotional state to reduce the likelihood of him becoming angry. As an adult, you remain hypervigilant to the emotional reactions of others. You behave in ways that try to minimize the distress of those around you. You also find the experience of anxiety intolerable. And when preparing to go out now, your mind and body remember the emotional state of fear and worry from that time.

Perhaps this latest episode of anxiety was triggered by some other stress in your life – challenges at work, relationship difficulties, or parenting fears. But whatever the issue, you remember the feeling. The anxiety is stored in your body and mind. And when you feel it, you quickly revert to the trauma pattern that got you through in the past. It's adaptive. Though not necessarily conscious of it, you've developed a behavioral strategy of avoiding that emotional experience. Now you've recognized that this strategy is unhelpful.

In fact, anxiety often has a compounding effect over time. Each time you avoid something, it becomes more and more difficult to claw your way back to doing that same thing the next time. That's why, by the time people come for psychological help, they're often very limited in their lives at that stage. And the treatment? Exposure to the anxiety itself, usually within the context of CBT (cognitive behavioral therapy). However, in my view, exposure treatment without a full understanding of anxiety across your lifetime and its context is unlikely to work in the long term.

This is why psychological formulation is so crucial. In reading this book, you're going to learn to build your own unique formulation and see the power of telling your story, even if only to yourself. (*For a fuller explanation of what I mean by 'formulation,' see page 133.*) For some of you, the issue might be low mood. For others, something else. Whatever the presenting issue – the problems that caused you to seek help – I view that as the symptom and I want to get the root of it. And we cannot get to the root without digging deeper.

Now, before you can start to build your own psychological formulation, you need to understand a couple of key concepts and theories. The first concept is that a good psychological formulation is undertaken within a biopsychosocial framework. This means that biological, psychological, and social aspects are all taken into account. The biopsychosocial model considers each of these areas and the interaction between them in the understanding of health and illness. It adds to the holistic picture we need when trying to understand our own psychology.

The next two concepts that are crucial for us to understand are attachment theory and social learning theory. First proposed by the British psychologist John Bowlby in 1969, attachment theory is the foundation upon which relational therapies are built. (Social learning theory is also relational, in that it describes how we learn by imitation. But let's start with attachment.) Attachment is the process by which a baby bonds emotionally with, and responds to, its earliest caregivers. It's a survival mechanism to ensure that an infant builds close emotional ties to its mother (or other primary caregiver), and therefore ensures its survival as she seeks to meet its needs for nutrition, comfort, and security. More widely, attachment is the process by which all human beings learn how to relate to themselves and others.

Social learning theory, put simply, is all about modeling. Proposed by the Canadian-American psychologist Albert Bandura in 1977, social learning theory outlines the importance of observation and copying what we see in order to learn new things. This extends to our relationships. We grow up looking to and observing the adults around us. We see how they interact with, and relate to, others. We see how they interact with the self and we see how they interact with and relate to us. In this way, we develop a practical model of how relationships work and we then use that model repeatedly in our day-to-day lives.

> The problem is that sometimes the modeling we receive can be unhelpful.

This can mean that we end up utilizing a relationship blueprint that is flawed, over and over again. Later, we'll explore this in more detail and consider what has been modeled to you that is perhaps still impacting you today.

Now, typically, the process of assessment and formulation, utilizing psychological knowledge and theories, including attachment and social learning theory, is undertaken through working with a psychologist or some other therapist. In good therapy, that formulation or 'story' will be presented to the person to check it resonates with their experience. And it isn't set in stone.

Your psychological formulation should similarly be ever-evolving and dynamic.

After all, life carries on regardless, even when we're struggling to cope with the daily demands that are placed on us.

Emerging

My daughter returned to school seven weeks after her dad died. The summer holidays had afforded us time as a family to love each other and grieve privately. Now the prospect of public separation loomed. As we arrived at the school playground that morning, I sensed this wasn't going to go as I'd hoped. Simply turning up at school that morning had been challenging for me, as we ran the gauntlet of people looking to convey condolences and ask unwelcome questions. I had to turn one person away, saying something like, 'Now is not the time.' I knew that if people enquired or even mentioned what had happened to me, I would break down.

I can only imagine what sense my little girl was making of it all. She was just five years old, had lost her daddy only weeks before, and now she was being expected to separate from her one remaining parent, be placed in the care of her new teacher, and then spend time with other children, who might ask her about what had happened in much the same way that I'd been interrogated on my way through the school gates. As the other kids lined up to start primary two, my little one clung to me. I didn't force her into line in full view of everyone. Instead, I let the rest of her class go inside and then took her to the school office reception area. There I sat with her, stroking her hand, reassuring and reminding her how important it was to get back into a routine and see her friends again.

I was so grateful when a good friend of mine who is a very experienced pupil support worker came to take her into class.

This was an adult my daughter knew well outside school and had a bond with. Someone I trusted implicitly. Despite this, as my little girl was encouraged to leave me, she became upset. I was prompted to go and naturally she became even more vocal – distressed even. It took everything in me not to go to her, pull her close, and take her home, but I knew that would only delay the inevitable. This is the agonizing paradox of parenting, I think: building as secure an attachment with your child as you can, but also knowing when separation is important and necessary.

Despite my logic, as I walked across the school playground with tears streaming down my face, I felt like the worst mother in the world. Perhaps you disagree with my method, but as parents we're all simply trying to do our best, and my rationale – that it was helpful to have my daughter back in school – felt right to me. I should also say that I'd previously met with the head teacher and her new teacher prior to the beginning of term. We were particularly blessed with a teacher who had herself lost a parent as a child and who was incredibly sensitive to our plight. We agreed on several strategies to allow my daughter to grieve and express her needs during school hours, should she need to. This included time out with her best friend.

I tell this story to illustrate attachment in action. My daughter and I have a secure attachment. It was evident when she was asked to separate from me after our collective family trauma. In many ways, I'm sure it seems counter-intuitive to assume that her distress is the indicator of secure attachment. But the real test is that though distressed at the point of separation, she was waiting for me happily at the school pick-up and had learned an incredibly valuable lesson that day. Sure, as her mum, I could make her feel safe and secure, particularly after a trauma like the one we'd experienced. However, the real lesson was that she could separate from me and cope with her distress, as she emerged from the cocoon that had been our family home since her dad's death. She did this through seeking comfort from other attuned adults, and coping with how she felt in an age-appropriate way, in the knowledge that I would always be there for her to come home to. Her secure base.

My own emergence from that cocoon began with the funeral. The time between Matty's death and the funeral had felt endless. A limbo land of 17 arduous days of grief and paperwork, planning, and the relentless feeling of responsibility that came with three small children now depending solely on me. I wrote his eulogy through the fog of it all.

When the day came, my heart was wounded and weary. I chose not to have the children present, as I felt instinctively that I would have to focus on my own needs that day. They were also very young and I didn't believe it would be helpful, as their understanding was so limited. I arranged to have a friend pick them up in the morning. She was a primary school teacher, and I knew she would be another adult I could depend on to attune to my children's emotional needs – and I was grateful.

I spent the morning largely alone, getting ready to lay my husband to rest. There were moments when I questioned whether I could face it. How could I stand by passively as he was lowered into the ground? I hated the feeling that I would be on show in front of a full church. The same little stone church in which we and my parents before us had said our marriage vows: 'Till death do us part.' I imagined that people would be watching me, scrutinizing my facial expressions and emotions, with expectations of a certain reaction. But I swallowed it all down and got on with doing what needed to be done.

When I arrived at the church and climbed out of the funeral car, my mum came to meet me. Suddenly, I had a flashbulb memory of myself eight years earlier, arriving in my Swarovski-encrusted wedding dress at this very same spot, driven with my dad in a vintage Rolls-Royce Silver Cloud, my mum waiting for us in her green outfit with a feather in her hat. I wonder now if she had a similar memory. As she approached me in the churchyard, she asked, 'Do you want your dad?' as if he needed to take me on this walk down the aisle of the church, just like before. My response was immediate and visceral. 'No,' I replied as she took my arm. 'I want you.' I wanted my mum. My secure base.

Emotional Inhibition

I've previously highlighted how in my early grief, my emotions felt difficult to access. And when I did access them, they felt overwhelming. The reason was that I was doing a good job of inhibiting my emotional response most of the time. Some of this was, of course, practical. Through my grief, I continued to care for my three children, getting them to school and their childminder each day. Feeding, clothing, bathing, and loving them meant I couldn't be constantly at the mercy of my emotions. I simply couldn't stand there weeping in the street or school playground. There were very real things to do and tasks to complete.

I also think that when we allow ourselves to feel the emotion, it makes the event that has invited the response all the more real. In my case, and in many of my clients' cases, we would rather deny what has happened or minimize its impact on us.

Denial is protective, until it no longer is.

I think, subconsciously, I worried that if I allowed myself to express my grief fully, there was a chance it might destroy me. And I couldn't afford to let that happen.

There were times where I tried to allow space for my emotions to come through. Once the children were out of the house, I'd intentionally keep the curtains drawn, slump to the floor, and just sob and sob. It was a welcome release of pent-up sorrow. I felt wretched and these momentary episodes gave me some relief.

However, on several occasions, this process was interrupted by someone coming to the front door. If I could, I would simply hide, though that wasn't always possible. Reflecting on it now, I was ashamed of the unbridled force of my emotions. I worried that people would take this as a sign that I wasn't coping and was therefore unable to look after my children. I worried that I looked unhinged. Irrational thinking, perhaps, but it felt real to me. So, I would quickly dry my tears and splash my face with water, and hope I didn't come across as someone who was losing control when I opened the door and forced a smile. Isn't it ridiculous that even during one of the most traumatic events of my life, I was concerned my emotions might mean something was wrong with me, or that my response would be 'too much' for other people to cope with?

Now, this is the singularly most common challenge I see in clinical practice. Regardless of the problem people come to the therapy room with, their age, culture or background, they are often keen to inhibit their natural emotional responses. Why? Well, for so many reasons. Because society has historically told us that emotions signal weakness. Because we feel shameful and vulnerable when our underbelly is exposed. And because, far too often, emotions have remained unspoken in our homes or even maligned by our parents, who were themselves ill-equipped to deal with their emotions and so the emotions of their children, in turn.

What happens to those of us who were raised in this way? Usually it leaves us with a dearth of emotional language and an inability to tune in to our emotional world. Our emotional guidance system has essentially been shut down and we're forced to live largely unaware of, and numbed out to, our feelings. When those feelings become too much and break through, as they inevitably will, we develop unhelpful coping strategies to compensate. We find ever more elaborate ways to build our numbing capabilities.

Overeating or undereating and using alcohol or drugs are all strategies that remove our feelings, even if only temporarily. These strategies help absolve us of our responsibility for our feelings, too. Sometimes, strategies give us a sense of pleasure, when we seek to emphasize positive feelings to drown out the harder-to-feel emotions. We use pleasurable experiences as a tool to feel good. Things that give us a dopamine hit are common – scrolling through social media, sex, drinking too much coffee, and gaming for hours are just some of the behaviors in which we may engage in order to cope.

> Ultimately, so many of us struggle with accessing our emotional plane because we've never been taught how.

Given that our parents before us perhaps weren't taught either, this creates the very definition of a vicious cycle. Many of us never realize the extent of our difficulties with emotional attunement until we experience a larger trauma that unearths it.

MINDFUL ATTUNEMENT PRACTICE

Before you move on to Chapter 3, I'd like you to start doing some work on emotional attunement. To know ourselves better and cultivate self-awareness, it's crucial to develop our capacity for this.

I'd therefore like you to spend some time putting together your own individualized mindful attunement practice. In order to make this something you can feasibly do each day, I'd like you to consider a few key things before developing a practice that works for you.

1. What time of the day is most feasible for you to incorporate this practice into your daily life?

2. What length of time feels enough and won't become a chore? (This can be as little as three to five minutes.)

3. How can you ensure that you remember in your busy daily life to attune to your current emotional state? Perhaps you could set an alarm on your phone? Or could you build in your 'time to attune' after lunch or another meal? This will help you to stack this new habit on top of something you already do, making it easier to incorporate it into your schedule.

4. In your journal, write a short script that talks you through questions that tap into how you are feeling emotionally. I've offered an example of an attunement script below, to support you. You can also download this from my website as an audio file for your phone and play it back throughout the day, or whenever you need to attune. (You can download the audio file at the following link www.drlaurawilliams.com/attunement).

Example emotional attunement script

Take a moment to ground yourself and breathe. Find a comfortable position either sitting or lying down, and place your hands comfortably in your lap or across your belly.

Begin by taking a deep breath in, filling your lungs and holding it at the top, before letting it out slowly for a few seconds. Sigh it out. I wonder if that's the deepest breath you've taken today? Notice how your body feels just by nourishing it with life-giving oxygen. Spend a few moments here breathing in and out and regulating your breath. There is nothing you need to do in this moment – just breathe.

And now, from this place, I want you to become aware of your emotional state. Simply by giving ourselves a few minutes each day to attune to how we feel emotionally, we can make a difference to our psychological well-being. That's all it takes.

So, how do you feel today? Are you sad? Do you feel low? Or is your mood elevated and upbeat? Are you angry or preoccupied? Do you feel overwhelmed? Once you've identified what emotion is present for you in this moment, repeat this phrase to yourself out loud: 'I feel [whatever emotion you've identified] today.' (So, for example, you might say, 'I feel sad today.') Say it now. Take care to ensure it's an emotion, rather than a thought that you've picked out.

Now, allow yourself a few moments to really 'feel' it. Rather than suppressing your emotion, or distracting yourself from it, just allow yourself to feel. Emotions come and go. You won't always feel the way you do in this moment, and by allowing yourself to feel, you will help your emotions move on through.

And with your emotional state identified, I want you to consider what has led you to feel this way. What has been happening in your life that might offer some clues to your current emotional state? Have you been struggling in your relationships? Has something good happened at work? Are you feeling particularly connected or disconnected from those around you? The goal here is simply to get curious and begin to make the links between your emotions and life events. Emotional attunement is like a muscle. If you practice it daily, you will get better at it in time.

Finally, slowly allow yourself to return to the room. Attuning to your emotional state is likely to mean that you will meet your needs better today. So, go into your day, knowing that you have prioritized your emotions and your needs.

CHAPTER 3

Leaving Old
You Behind

After my first degree in psychology, I was lucky enough to secure a job straight out of university with the Scottish Prison Service. My summer work experience as a student in the Young Offenders Institute at Polmont had definitely helped me to secure a permanent post. This sort of position had been my dream for years and I vividly remember taking the phone call to say that I'd got the post. The role was based at HMP Edinburgh, known locally as 'Saughton,' and involved delivering offending behavior programs.

I was unfazed at the time, but looking back I'm slightly baffled at my confidence and willingness to get stuck in to often harrowing work while I was so inexperienced and just 21 years old. I'd been told that this would be a valuable apprenticeship into psychological work and just a matter of weeks later, I was handing over my I.D. to gain entry behind those high walls, and completing the key and security training that would allow me to move around the jail freely.

The group programs I facilitated in the prison involved using cognitive behavioral therapy and principles to unlock the puzzle of why these men had offended in the first place, and how they might help themselves desist in the future. One of the exercises that we asked offenders to complete within the program was called 'Background Factors,' which essentially involved working on understanding their unique psychological formulation. To do this, group members were asked to consider the experiences of their past and to set these out in a written piece of work if they were able to do so. They'd then come back to the group and present it by reading it aloud. Sometimes, if they were struggling to read it themselves, either because of overwhelming emotion or because they were fearful of the act of presenting itself, facilitators would read it for them.

These exercises never failed to move me and always invited compassionate feedback from the group members themselves. They were always stories of trauma and hardship – a jigsaw of many pieces laid out to reveal poor and volatile relationships, unhealthy attachments and fear. These men had endured much; their lives were blighted by their traumatic experiences. They themselves had gone on to treat others in ways that mirrored their own traumas, had been caught, and were now being punished by society.

The levels of shame that these men faced each day were palpable. You could see it in the way they carried themselves when they thought nobody was looking. It was particularly evident in the group of prisoners who refused to engage in therapeutic groups, because to do so would have meant acknowledging their guilt. These men were not incarcerated by high walls, heavy locked doors, or wide iron bars. Shame was their prison. They masked it with puffed-out chests and angry demeanors.

I've seen this replicated in the general population, too. Shame silences us. It makes us imagine we must be the only one to feel or behave the way we do, so we continue to live an inauthentic life, masking our true selves behind the layers of what's gone before. (*We'll be taking a closer look at shame in Chapter 8.*)

> I wonder how many of us understand the impact shame has had on us – how it locks us up on the inside and throws away the key.

Old Me, New Me

Given the position these men were in, it was no easy task to get them to undertake psychological work. Psychologists in these roles were often eyed with suspicion and wariness. Yet it was clear that to 'progress' through the prison estate, offenders were expected to engage in programs. Essentially, if they wanted to get along, be afforded privileges and to be seen playing by the rules, engaging in programs was an integral part of that process. This meant that a power dynamic existed between the psychologists who ran them and those we sought to rehabilitate.

Many men didn't want to do the work, but realized it was their bargaining chip. However, as mentioned, engaging in programs meant engaging with guilt and telling their story, and I believe some of them found the process fairly excruciating. What that meant was that many would show up, but their participation could be superficial.

> The instinct for self-protection is strong, particularly in those who have been traumatized.

To combat this lack of willingness, a further concept was introduced within the group – of 'Old Me, New Me.' This was an incredibly helpful approach to the work, as it introduced the notion that leaving behind the old version of yourself was indeed possible. Moreover, the exercise allowed group members to begin rewriting the narrative of their lives and to invest belief in what was possible for them in the future. It began to scaffold their psychological awareness and allowed them to start visualizing a different reality for themselves.

One of the reasons that psychological work and therapy can be so challenging is that you are being asked to examine the parts of yourself that you don't like very much, and then to allow them to die. I think this mostly helped the offenders I engaged with as it allowed them to detach from who they had been. However, change is desperately hard for so many reasons. First, it takes courage and tenacity to look inward and acknowledge our flaws. Many of us find it so threatening that we defend against it, building high walls of denial around ourselves. Then, if we get past that stage, it takes discipline and consistency to override the natural and well-worn behavioral responses of our past. Allowing parts of ourselves that have reliably kept us safe to wither can feel intolerable – as if the essential building blocks of what made us ourselves are crumbling apart.

Some simply stop at this juncture. They cannot cope with the emotional discomfort and shame that this sort of work induces. The question is, what would you do? Are you willing to spend your own valuable time looking inward, peeling back the layers of your psychological makeup, and understanding what you can let go of? Identifying the limitations that your past experiences have placed on you? If you are ready to do this work, I want you to know that though it might not feel like it in the beginning, it will empower you. It will revitalize your sense of self and purpose, and it will set you free from whatever version of a personal prison that you have been living in.

Traumatic Loss

Many of you, like me, will have experienced a loss. Some of you may not. However, loss is a universal experience. Even in the absence of the death of a loved one, loss exists in many guises. It's present in separation and divorce, loss of friendships, or loss of a job or identity. I've also worked with those who struggle with the loss of their own independence, or of their children as they leave the nest. The loss of the childhood we perhaps wish we could have had is particularly poignant.

My own loss was sudden and traumatic. Traumatic loss has been defined as any experience of loss that involves your previously held assumptions of how the world operates, how people should behave, and how you view yourself (Kauffman, 2002). Other researchers go further and say that these core assumptions are 'shattered' by a traumatic loss (Janoff-Bulman, 1992). But the route into this work does not discriminate. There is no yardstick for whether you meet the criteria for building self-awareness and embracing self-development. You are here today, in this moment, reading these words because you want to understand your psychology better.

This is one of the most fascinating aspects of my work, I think. Among all the evidence-based practice in which clinical psychology is grounded, there is a universal truth. And this is that a person's individual experience is determined not by what the textbooks tell us about it, but by their own perception of it.

Trauma is perceived on an individual basis, and what one person finds traumatic, another may not.

Many of the men I worked with in the prison genuinely didn't perceive their experience to be at all traumatic. The way they had lived and survived had been the norm for them. And so, when a 21-year-old psychologist, with limited experience of both life and the work, knocks on your cell door and asks you to talk about your trauma, it can not only appear threatening but perhaps even be perceived as condescending. This created yet another barrier for me to overcome.

As I write this, I recall a woman I worked with several years ago who had experienced a tremendous amount of neglect in her upbringing. There had been a lack of access to food, comfort, and emotional stability. Despite regularly being left alone to fend for herself, she hadn't perceived this as neglect, and neither had anybody else. Her family were relatively affluent and her parents were both in positions of authority and trust. Behind closed doors, the reality was very different to the outer veneer, but no one could see her pain. Crucially, neither could she.

Through gentle exploration and sensitive enquiry, she recalled how when she was in a school setting at the age of about 11, a teacher recognized her lack of socialization at mealtimes. This woman had never been taught to use a knife and fork, nor how to eat with others. The teacher was compassionate and began scaffolding her skills from the bottom up. It was this recollection, uncovered during therapy, that was the moment when it finally all made sense to her. The trauma and the neglect she had experienced were real. The impact it had had on her became so much more obvious when she had allowed herself the chance to tell her story, and really hear and see it for the first time as an adult. As she sat opposite me, stunned, her tears began to fall. Just as the men in the jail viewed their life as normal, so did this woman – until she self-validated through therapeutic work. She had finally understood all that she had lost.

Jo's Story

Jo's story was similar to my own, in that she'd lost her husband in sudden and traumatic circumstances. She'd come across me one day while listening to Connie McLaughlin's Sunday-morning program on Radio Scotland. I'd been invited on the show to talk about coping with grief.

Despite her overwhelming loss and the emotional fallout from it, Jo was warm and engaged. She seemed self-assured and confident that she was here with me in therapy to begin processing her bereavement. However, she was clear that she didn't wish to discuss her history before the loss, as it wasn't relevant, so we began where she was comfortable. Telling the story of her husband's loss, often in forensic detail, allowed Jo to release a lot of emotion that had been suppressed. She, like me, had been 'a coper' and so the emotion had taken a back seat for a time.

One afternoon, Jo's husband had gone out walking with their beloved family dogs, but he hadn't arrived home as expected. When Jo couldn't get in touch with him, she began to feel uneasy. She jumped into her car and drove to where she knew he had gone. As the story unfolded, she talked of an inner knowing that something terrible had happened. I've heard many stories of trauma over the years and, in a similar way to myself and many of my previous clients, Jo's intuition came to the fore. When she arrived at the location and saw police officers present, she knew her worst fears had been realized. The police told Jo her husband was gone.

The detail with which she recounted her story was not unusual, either. This is how 'flashbulb' memories work.

If the memory holds significant meaning, it tends to be etched into our memory store in a way that other, less significant memories aren't. That's why we remember events like our first day at school, a special birthday, or the death of a loved one. It's the meaning that makes the memory stick — not whether it would be considered a positive or negative one.

Even events largely external to our own lives can hold significance, and flashbulb memories of them are laid down. Notable examples for me that you may share too are the death of Princess Diana, the terrorist attack on the twin towers in New York, and the first bombs of the Iraq war. These events might be considered a collective trauma. We can often remember the exact place or the people we were with when we heard of these events or watched them unfold on television.

This is how individual trauma memories work, too, of course. The traumatic event holds much significance and, whether we like it or not, it molds and reshapes how we understand and view ourselves, the world, and the future. This is known as Beck's Cognitive Triad, after the American psychiatrist Aaron Beck. Trauma interrupts our trajectory and forces us to re-evaluate the core aspects of who we are, how we think, and how we behave. Often, we come away with a more negative appraisal than what we had held before. At least for a time.

Jo was, of course, devastated by her loss, describing her husband as the only man she had been able to depend on in her whole life. As we continued to walk through her story, I gently began to thread into the conversation how our responses to traumatic events like the one she had experienced are in fact shaped by our history. Tentatively, she began to acknowledge that her childhood had in fact encouraged emotional suppression; that her experiences had taught her how to 'cope' in the world, and that these strategies were not always adaptive.

Jo had grown up in a Catholic family in an area 45 minutes north of Belfast in Northern Ireland, against the backdrop of the Troubles. She acknowledged that she grew up 'living in a culture of fear,' often not knowing what would happen next. Jo was the seventh sibling in a family of eight children, and times were difficult, with the five girls sharing one bedroom. Jo's mother worked hard at looking after her children, though Jo noted that her mother made it clear to her that she had never wanted to have so many of them. Jo's father had struggled with his mental health and in the height of the conflict in Belfast, had disappeared for weeks. Jo acknowledged her fear of him when she was a child, stating that he was an angry man.

As an adult, she was able to reflect on the past and thought that having so many children had placed a degree of pressure on both of her parents, as they worked hard to provide a life for them all. Through the upbringing that she had, Jo had learned that emotions were not to be spoken of. Now, Jo was able to work through her history, acknowledging how she had been conditioned as a child. The patterns present in her childhood meant that as an adult she often tried to appease people by fawning. Fawning is essentially the behavioral strategy of consistently meeting others' needs at the expense of our own in order to avoid disapproval and criticism. This was something she had also seen modeled by her mother. Jo felt that her mother had in many ways martyred herself, but though she seemed resigned to the reality of her life, she wasn't necessarily unhappy.

When I asked Jo to tell me what understanding her psychology better had allowed her to do, she said this: 'The thing I resisted the most – looking at my psychology, my childhood, and my patterns – was the thing I needed to do to give me the answers and the way through my grief and my pain. My childhood does still have an impact on me now. My mother worked herself into the ground to look after others, to the point of exhaustion and suffering. I now know that wasn't a healthy choice and I can choose to stop replicating it through people-pleasing. The modeling I received doesn't have to inform my patterns and behaviors forever. I can interrupt those patterns and choose to behave differently myself.'

Jo's words encapsulate her struggle with vulnerability. Only when she felt safe enough to lean in and look, was the route map through her grief gradually revealed to her. Jo needed to allow herself to share, feel, and have her emotions validated; something she hadn't been encouraged to do in childhood. She also acknowledged how she subjugated her own needs in order to please others. Through developing her psychological mindedness and self-awareness, Jo began to meet her own needs first. This was incredibly important in helping her move through the grief process.

In many ways, simply by allowing herself the opportunity to engage in therapy and have her grief witnessed by someone else, Jo started meeting needs that she may well have denied herself in the past. One of the most poignant things Jo ever said to me during our work together was how tired she felt of grieving. In one of our last sessions together she concluded, 'I miss him. I miss my team.' I knew just how she felt.

Gratitude

In the early days and months after my husband's death, family, friends, and people who were strangers to me rallied around, taking my children on days out, sending me meal vouchers to fill my freezer or messages of heartfelt condolence. It was overwhelming to feel held in mind by so many people. Being 'held in mind' is one of the key messages that I try as a psychologist to convey to my clients. It means: You are important. Your experience and what you are going through matters. Even when I am not with you, you're held in my mind.

My reaction to the seemingly unending support I received from my network was an upsurge in gratitude. It appeared almost unfathomable to me that, at a time when I was so desperately sad and struggling to imagine how life could go on this way without him, I also felt so immensely grateful. We often forget that positive and negative emotions can coexist. In fact, my grief and my gratitude not only coexisted, they were codependent and neither could have existed without the other.

I was grieving hard because of what my life had been like before and my immense gratitude for it. My gratitude for that life and the years we'd shared, as well as the love that now surrounded me, was in a strange way enhanced by the gravity of the loss itself. My gratitude at that time was so evident, because we had suffered this loss. It was an intense feeling I'd never quite experienced before. It bubbled up inside of me, molten and raw, filling up my heart. It was like an emotional tidal wave, which sent me looking for the theory that would back it up.

The positive experience of my gratitude
propelled me forward and allowed me
to imagine that not only could life go
on, but aspects of it could be better
because we had suffered this loss.

I believe this was the beginning of my journey through post-traumatic growth.

Post-Traumatic Growth

Positive psychological growth after traumatic loss seems counterintuitive, I know. I don't wish you to make the mistake of thinking that I'm minimizing my loss or anyone else's traumatic life events. I will grieve forever. That much I know. But never again would I take this life for granted. Never again would I make myself smaller, dimming my light and my purpose within this world. In the depths of my sadness a new version of me was being born. One in which I felt more self-assured, confident, and worthy.

These positive psychological changes reflect the growth I experienced due to my traumatic loss.

Through struggle and hardship, we
begin to foster resilience and growth.

Post-traumatic growth (PTG), first defined by researchers in 1995, is the positive psychological change experienced as a result of the struggle with highly challenging life circumstances (Calhoun and Tedeschi, 1999, 2001). PTG occurs when positive psychological changes arise from the hardship and struggles that we face across our lives. Trauma literally becomes our teacher or coach.

It's a bit like the way your muscles grow in size and strength when you expose them to the stress of a strength program, adapting to a new reality day by day, training session after training session. Researchers have also noted that PTG encompasses five key domains. These include personal strength, changing priorities, improved relationships, changed philosophies, and spiritual development (Calhoun and Tedeschi, 1996, 2004). Personally, I noticed shifts in each of these areas and my life has been enriched as a consequence. I can only speak for myself here, but knowing that in our darkest moments we are often opened up to the light that is present all around us, gives me great comfort.

Together, throughout this book, we will walk through an evaluation of your psychology and how it's been shaped. As we conclude this first part of the book, I'd like you to consider these two versions of yourself. Firstly, the 'old' version of you who has been living in ways that perhaps don't support your psychological well-being. Secondly, the 'new' version of you that you are working toward. After completion of this exercise and the first part of this book, you'll be ready to move on to explore with me the truth about trauma, as I see it, and begin applying these learnings to your own experiences.

OLD ME, NEW ME EXERCISE

The wonderful thing about this exercise is that you get to rewrite the narrative of your life, going forward. I want you to focus first on the here and now, and then, secondly, on your future.

Set aside some time and get out your journal or notebook. Essentially, you are going to tell the story of 'old me' and the 'new me' you are hoping to create, using the writing prompts below to guide you:

'Old me' writing prompts

- *How did you live as 'old me' in the past?*

- *How did you feel as 'old me'?*

- *Who were you spending your time with and what impact was that having?*

- *How was your mental health?*

- *How was your physical health?*

- *What maladaptive or unhelpful coping strategies were you utilizing then? (This could include avoidance, use of substances to 'numb out' or throwing yourself into a relationship in the belief that this would 'fix' the problem. It will of course be individual.)*

- *How have your past experiences impacted who you are today?*

'New me' writing prompts

- *How would you like to be living?*

- *How would you like to feel?*

- *Who will this new version of yourself spend time with and what impact will that have?*

- *How will your mental health be positively impacted as you embrace 'new me'?*

- *How will your physical health be positively impacted as you become 'new me'?*

- *What alternative coping strategies will you use as 'new me'?*

- *How have your past experiences promoted your post-traumatic growth?*

PART II

The Truth About Trauma

CHAPTER 4

What Makes Us Who We Are

Attachment is a concept that is strongly linked to childhood relationships. As described earlier, it's the close bond formed between a child and its principal caregiver as they learn to relate to one another. The attachment dyad, or pairing, can comprise a father, daughter, mother, son, or any other composition of relationship in which the child is interacted with and looked after by a primary caregiver. For some, this may have been a grandparent, foster parent, or another adult.

But what is attachment really? In this chapter, we're going to learn how attachment is not only something that psychologists pay attention to in childhood, but a process that continues to influence how we relate to ourselves and others as adults on a lifelong basis. I think of attachment as a relational imprinting – a style and pattern of relating to others, modeled by our parents, and printed upon our blank pages. This makes sense, as we learn through observing those around us. They show us what to do and how to do it. We learn language and communication, turn-taking, and reciprocity – the intricate dance of reciprocal interaction that goes back and forth.

Similarly, we learn what not to do through negative reinforcement, when the reactions we get are less than favorable. And we learn through positive reinforcement to repeat things for which we are praised and receive a favorable response. A positive response from those around us makes it more likely we will repeat that behavior, while a negative response makes it more likely that we will let the behavior go.

This childhood conditioning is important, though often unseen. I can't tell you how many times I've worked with adults who struggle to make any conscious link between their 'here and now' problems and difficulties, and what their childhood conditioning and attachment relationships were like. Part of the reason for this, I believe, is that much of our conditioning is nonverbal. For example, it may take the form of a look that communicates a thousand words or feelings. Perhaps we see that look and it tells us that our parent or caregiver is disappointed, angry, sad, or tired. Like a sponge, we keep soaking in all this information about our principal caregiver's emotional state, and adjusting ourselves and our behavioral responses in line with what we are seeing.

Remember that attachment is a survival mechanism to make sure we will be looked after on an ongoing basis. And even when our parent's or other principal caregiver's expectations are communicated verbally, it doesn't necessarily follow that we can make the links between then and now. This is why I want to make that therapeutic process of understanding the link between the past and the present simpler for you. When the processes underpinning these difficulties are so nuanced and challenging to separate out, as humans trying to make sense of things, we simply don't make the connections that aid our understanding.

The Process of Attachment

Bowlby's theory of attachment points out that as infants we are born with an innate set of attachment behaviors, which are designed to ensure that the adult attachment figures around us will keep us safe from physical and psychological threats, encourage us to safely explore our environments, and help us to regulate our emotions well (Bowlby, 1969, 1982). These attachment behaviors are infant responses such as crying when we are in need as babies. Perhaps we're cold and we need a blanket. Perhaps we're hungry and need to be fed. Perhaps we're scared and we need to feel safe and secure again. What's important is how an infant's needs are responded to. As a clinician working with those who are managing some sort of psychological difficulty in adulthood, I often find that there can be a number of core needs left unmet in the childhoods of these people. And if this applies to you, too, and your needs for physical and emotional safety and security weren't met when you were little, then you will operate in the world in a way that reflects those early experiences.

> If you didn't feel safe and secure as a child, you will crave whatever feels safe and secure for you in the here and now.

AMY'S STORY

When I first met Amy, she told me that over the previous year things had been getting on top of her. She acknowledged she had a strong inner self critic, which had been affecting her time with her children and her intimacy with her husband. She had been aware for over a decade that she 'didn't like herself,' and that she struggled with anxiety and poor body image. Her difficulties with her body image meant she shied away from wearing clothes that revealed her body in any way. This was particularly challenging in summer when the expectation arose for her to wear vest tops, shorts, or a swimming costume, which then increased her anxiety further.

During the pandemic lockdown, Amy had been aware of gaining some weight and had got into a pattern of what she described as heavy eating at night, followed by restriction the next day. Though never formally diagnosed with an eating disorder, Amy was clear that a cycle of bingeing and restriction and occasional attempts at making herself sick had emerged. Amy also weighed herself frequently to keep track and wanted to stay around eight stone – an arbitrary but meaningful cut-off weight for her.

More recently, Amy's family had experienced a sudden and traumatic bereavement. She had reacted as many people do under such circumstances and had gone into what she termed 'help mode,' as she tried to support the wider family in their grief. This meant that she'd been unable to meet her own needs during this time, as she catered to the needs of others.

Amy's therapeutic goals were now to develop a healthier view of her body and physical appearance, improve her relationships with her children and other family members, and to understand her most prevalent patterns of not meeting her own needs and her disordered eating. Ultimately, Amy wanted to be more able to meet her needs as an adult in a healthy way.

When discussing her early life, Amy described her parents as down-to-earth and working class. She had one sister. In high school, Amy experienced bullying in her first year and noted that it was around this time that she began to eat more food as a form of comfort. From an early age, Amy remembered being compared to her sister, and in high school her sister had refused to converse with her, which in Amy's view was because she was 'an embarrassment.'

She remembered internalizing an idea that she was 'ugly' and 'not good enough.'

At around the same time, Amy's mum developed depression after her father, Amy's grandfather, died. Amy stated that by the time she left school to go to work, at the age of 16, she felt she was overweight, and a restrictive eating pattern had taken hold.

With regards to her relationships with her parents, Amy felt she was closest to her mum. However, Amy also acknowledged that her mum's love and approval felt conditional. She was, for example, required to behave and look a certain way to gain her mum's attention and affection. She didn't feel as connected to her dad, who tended to lack emotion and had a stoic, 'pull your socks up' attitude.

Within the family home, both of Amy's parents would shout during arguments. Occasionally this led to physical contact and pushing. This left Amy feeling angry and stuck, as she attempted to navigate these challenges. Clinically, it was evident that Amy had experienced a degree of parentification (where the parent–child roles are reversed) and she was at times looking after her mum by providing a sounding board for her negative feelings and depression. Consequently, Amy learned to put her mum's needs before her own, as a parent might, and this set in motion a pattern of her own needs being overlooked in the years to come.

As I think about Amy's case, I am reminded of something I learned during my training while working in child and adolescent mental health services. A supervisor once told me never to forget that we have very little control as children. This is why the difficulties that children present with to services can often show up in the areas where they *can* exert a degree of control, such as sleeping, toileting, and eating – areas in which they hold some autonomy over whether they choose to engage in the behavior we might want or expect of them.

Part of Amy's formulation of difficulties was that in her childhood and early teens she had struggled with her living situation and the lack of safety and security offered by her parents. Amy used eating and food initially to offer her the comfort, safety, and security she lacked within her relational environment. When she gained weight, attracting negative attention, Amy had then learned that she could also find that same safety and security in the control that the restriction of food offered. And so began the pendulum of her restrictive eating versus her binge eating. Years later, this maladaptive coping pattern had emerged again, offering stability when her life had felt similarly out of control. And the pattern of subjugating her own needs had never really gone away.

Over the course of my work with Amy, she began to communicate better with her husband, from whom she had largely hidden her eating difficulties and body-image fears. She had noticed how this communication had naturally led to a greater ease of intimacy between them, and they were better able to schedule time for each other. Inspired by her children, Amy had started to wear shorts, reminding herself that her body did not necessarily look 'bad' in the ways she believed it did. This allowed her to engage in activities with her children more freely.

Amy had previously shied away from having her photograph taken. This was something she felt sad about, as it meant she'd been unable to document her children's childhood fully in images that included her. Amy now embraces a 'daily selfie' – a challenge we devised collaboratively to expose her to visibility and increase her body positivity. She has also stopped weighing herself daily.

In relation to Amy's overarching pattern of subjugating her needs, the very act of coming to therapy was itself a step in a positive direction. Amy had also realized that she had been unhappy with her career. Though she had made the decision to change career prior to therapy commencing, I think she came to understand and trust through our work together that giving herself the freedom to meet her need for a change in her work was important for her overall happiness and fulfilment. Amy is now better able to meet her needs, whatever they are, without feeling quite so guilty, and I hope in time this pattern will become easier as she rewrites the narrative of her past.

Core Human Needs

We can't talk about needs without mentioning the American psychologist Abraham Maslow, who set out what he believed were basic and core human needs within his five-tier hierarchy of needs model (Maslow, 1954). At the bottom of the pyramid were physiological needs for food, water, oxygen, shelter, clothing, and sleep, forming the foundation upon which the remaining needs are built. The additional needs he highlighted were safety and security, love and belonging, self-esteem, and, at the top of the pyramid's hierarchy, self-actualization – the process of reaching your full potential. Self-actualization is considered the highest level of psychological development.

Maslow's premise was that our needs on the lower levels of the pyramid have to be met before the next levels up can be achieved. However, it isn't completely fixed and some variation will be present in what motivates us as individuals. Mostly, this model has helped the field of psychology put a framework around which needs are important and has allowed us to use this framework as a yardstick to understand any deficits in what we were offered as children.

Social Modeling Theory

In my view, no explanation of attachment can be complete without an understanding of social modeling theory (also known as social learning theory in the UK). This is the next step, in which we start to unravel how attachment becomes not simply a process in early infanthood, but a lifelong pattern of engagement in relationships. In 1969, Albert Bandura, a psychologist working out of Stanford University, explained that those working in the field of personality 'agreed that identification refers to a process in which a person patterns his thoughts, feelings or actions after another person who serves as a model' (Bandura, 1969, p.214).

Simply put, as we grow up we use the template or model provided to us by our early environment – that is, by our parents or primary caregivers. Though not consciously aware of it, the adults we live with become our template, teaching us the 'how to' of life and living. Inevitably, challenges can arise if those who we identify as being our teachers are delivering lessons that are skewed or flawed in some way. Often that is the result of their own internalized attachment model. In this way, we can begin to see the intergenerational nature of our psychology – the push down the generational line of unhelpful core beliefs, patterns of relating, and often psychological disorder itself.

Now, it's important to remind ourselves here that if those from whom we've taken our cues are thinking, feeling, or acting in ways that are unhelpful, we are of course unaware of this as children. We simply watch, learn, and recreate. As a consequence, we may begin to develop a repertoire of unhelpful behaviors that, over time, can leave us feeling disconnected, anxious, depressed, or sick – the opposite of what healthy attachment is designed to do. The ideal scenario is that healthy adults model and teach us the origins and building blocks of connection and security, leaving us with a legacy of robust mental well-being.

Additionally, attachment is powerful. That is why, even when we've had highly negative experiences with our loved ones, we can find it very hard to acknowledge this. This is adaptive from a survival point of view. We are supposed to want to remain connected to our people – because, at one point, our very survival depended on it. It's why, as adults, we may find it so challenging to reflect on, and think critically about, what we experienced when we were growing up. Anyone who has tried to open up conversations with a parent who we feel did not meet our core needs when we were young, will know the discomfort that this can create. That's attachment in action. It's still trying to ensure your 'survival' even now.

But here's the thing I need you to know: Even if you didn't receive security, love, and esteem as a child, you still can do as an adult.

When we realize that we're no longer in a survival situation and our internal threat

system can be safely deactivated, we can change the narrative for the better.

And we can do this by identifying our unmet needs and finding ways to fulfil them.

Personality Disorder

In my career as a clinical psychologist, I've worked with some of the most extreme expressions of psychological disorder and dysfunction, such as major depression, anxiety disorders, and eating disorders, to name a few. The common thread that runs through my clients' stories is one of disruptions or difficulties in the attachment relationship, and trauma.

Personality disorder is another area that I've worked in extensively. I've seen many times how the shadows of people's pasts show up and shape their personality structure in such a way that this creates major difficulties in their ability to relate to and connect authentically with others. Personality disorder is a tough diagnosis to receive. Many patients have talked to me about the lack of compassion and genuine empathy that they are met with when in receipt of the services set up to help them. In fact, not so long ago it used to be the case that personality disorder was considered 'not amenable to treatment.' In other words, we cannot do anything for you and you need to live your life alongside the disconnection and relational pain you experience. These patients were often treated with very little empathy, because their behaviors forced this disconnection. It's a heartbreaking form of self-sabotage to witness, and one born of that unmet need for a healthy attachment.

The disconnection that we can see, and often feel, when working with those who have attracted this label reflects clinicians' feelings of hopelessness and helplessness to foster meaningful change, and how hard it is to reach patients when their early attachments have been so disrupted. These days, things are changing – slowly. As clinicians, we're seeing a shift in how personality disorder is viewed. In particular, I welcome the changes in language, as we now seek to treat personality disorder as 'attachment difficulties' or 'complex trauma.' The links are evident and we now know that certain relational treatments such as Jeff Young's schema therapy or Anthony Ryle and Ian Kerr's cognitive analytic therapy (CAT) can be effective in working with this sector of the population.

Now, to be clear, most people don't present with this level of disorder or dysfunction in their lives. But that doesn't mean that they or you haven't experienced trauma of one form or another. Nor does it mean that they wouldn't benefit from taking a closer look at their own psychology through an attachment lens. And if it's true that we can now facilitate change over time in those who've been exposed to the most extreme examples of attachment difficulties and trauma, then, of course, you too can help yourself through building awareness and understanding, and by making changes in how you relate to yourself and others, wherever you fall on that spectrum.

Trauma Talks

Within the trauma work I do, anecdotally two groups of people emerge: those who struggle to acknowledge their past histories and those who are much more ready to do so. A culture is also developing in which trauma is often talked about by the latter group. Helpfully, people are becoming more comfortable with discussing their past trauma as the mental health conversation grows.

However, in parallel with the rise of this conversation on social media, it becomes unhelpful if sharing our traumatic histories isn't accompanied by an intention for change. The *Cambridge Dictionary* defines 'trauma dumping' as 'the act of telling another person or other people in a detailed way about problems and emotional pain that you have experienced.' Interestingly, this definition stops short of mentioning any action resulting from the sharing of traumatic experiences. Though we are talking about trauma more, and even coming up with new language and terms surrounding it, I'm not sure we're always aware as a collective of how the trauma we've experienced has impacted our behavior and, by extension, our relationships, and how we're perceived by others. And if we are not aware, how then do we know what we need to change?

This is a common problem in psychological work. Lack of insight and self-awareness of how trauma has affected us can push us to externalize responsibility, as we seek to apportion blame outside ourselves. This blame may be directed toward our parents or caregivers, partners or friends who, we believe, have further compounded our traumatic past through our experiences with them. However, I've repeatedly seen how blame leaves little room for taking personal responsibility or facilitating change. And please don't mistake my own view here as a lack of compassion. It's in fact the opposite. Often, it's the most traumatized in our midst who feel compelled to share their experiences openly, as they seek validation of their pain.

And their pain is real. Their early lived experience is part of the reason they behave as they do.

But we can't do what we haven't been taught. It's therefore challenging to take a responsible role in your own healing when you have been so influenced and impacted by the adults who you trusted to care for you and who perhaps took no responsibility for themselves. Yet, against the backdrop of this, it's incredibly important that we normalize not just talking about trauma but doing something about it.

Helping you to shift the shadows of what trauma has left behind is the aim of this book.

The other big problem is that the growing conversation online makes people scared of pulling back the curtain to look and really see. This issue is specific to that first group of people, who struggle to acknowledge their past because they either don't know to look in the first place, or are fearful to do so. I find this to be the case particularly with parents, who are scared they'll be told that they are 'damaging' their children by passing down these unhelpful ways of relating that they themselves learned. We can be so convinced of it that we simply avoid it.

It's also evident to me that because the online space often exposes us to those who have been most traumatized, this serves to minimize our own traumas. We compare our experience to that of strangers, and this renders us silent as we tell ourselves, 'My life wasn't so bad,' or, 'My parents did OK.' I'm not here to deny that reality. But, as I said earlier, trauma is not just about the 'big' things.

'Small t,' 'Big T' Trauma

In the United States, the language around trauma incorporates terms to explain its severity. This terminology is used less in a UK context, but I think it can be useful. The notion of 'big T' and 'small t' trauma highlights the idea that trauma isn't simply about the sort of extreme events that society often tells us it is. The big T's of childhood sexual abuse, neglect, or physical violence are well known; however, they are thankfully rarer than other causes. And what if you experienced none of these things, yet you still have a sense that your early experiences, and those that came after them, weren't especially helpful or healthy for your emotional development? It becomes even more confusing if you feel this, but also for the most part had loving and supportive parents.

My clinical practice has shown me time and again how trauma exists on a spectrum. Like a normal curve, those who have experienced the more extreme 'big T' trauma, or no trauma at all, number far fewer than those who have experienced levels of trauma that fit somewhere around the middle of that bell curve. What this means is that there are likely large numbers of people who have experienced 'small t' trauma, yet who have never acknowledged it.

These traumatized people include most of us, and though we may have experienced a 'lower level' of difficulty, it still impacts our lives.

However, the ways in which trauma affects us may remain imperceptible to us if we choose not to look. Think about those individuals you may have come across in the workplace, who are challenging to be around. The energy they give off can feel toxic and their behavior can sometimes match. It's likely that these people are influenced by their relationships from the past and trauma. They simply either don't see it, or are unable to effect change even if they do – something that I was to learn the hard way.

When I worked in prisons, I delivered a long-term offending behavior program focused on violence prevention. I was young, keen, and this was a crucial part of offender rehabilitation. I was delighted to be getting exposure to this type of work and I took my responsibility seriously. I also knew that things had to be done a certain way. The program was seven months long and it was important to ensure the right offenders were prioritized for it, so there was a selection process for the group, and I and two other prison officer facilitators conducted interviews to assess the inmates for suitability.

During this process, I became aware that the two other officers had completed several assessments that I felt weren't as detailed as they could have been, and I worried that something crucial had been missed. Then, following those assessments, and without discussion as a team, it was decided that several prisoners didn't need to complete the program. These were not insignificant decisions and I felt torn about what to do. I was concerned about the reliability of the assessments and how final decisions were being taken without wider consultation. I was also keenly aware of the importance of getting these decisions right and knew how key collaboration was in situations like this.

I raised my concerns with my own psychological supervisor, who agreed with me. Unsurprisingly, the two officers didn't take kindly to the challenge when my concerns were put to them by their own supervisor. This started a workplace experience that affected me for many years to come. Though I still had to work with these officers every day, they barely spoke to me and made it abundantly clear that they were unhappy both with my raising of the issues and with working with me. It meant that preparation for the group was difficult at best and almost nonexistent at worst.

As a result of me talking to my supervisor about the issue, they also raised a formal grievance against me. They claimed that I was bullying them because I'd questioned their work. I'd just turned 23 years old and these were two individuals with much longer service histories than me, who I had called out. I believed wholeheartedly that the decisions were ill-advised, and felt justified that I was simply being thorough and making sure that the selection process was conducted to a high standard. Yet every day I felt intimidated and sick to my stomach as I walked the short distance to the programs unit, locking and unlocking the solid metal doors as I went. Bullying was neither my intention nor how I was behaving in reality.

Ultimately, I was encouraged by supportive colleagues to file my own grievance, as they could see where the bullying behavior was actually originating. It was the hardest year in a post I've ever experienced to date. I left the prison service shortly afterwards, but not before completing the entire program. Moving to the NHS, where things were so different, I felt relieved to have escaped the toxicity and stress that I'd been exposed to.

The question I've asked myself while reflecting on this experience was about where my responsibility lay in what happened. Was I really bullying these people? Of course not. However, what was it about my actions that triggered their response? I know that what I did was right – technically. But could I have gone about it differently? Probably. Would that have ensued a different outcome? Now, that remains unclear.

What I do know for sure is that my need as a psychologist early in her career to make sure everything was done correctly, and 'by the book,' clashed with the officers' belief that they were right and more experienced than I was in their assessment of potential group members. I had been driven by my perfectionism and the need to be thorough. They were driven by the discomfort caused by their perception that they'd been criticized by a younger, less experienced, and more idealistic colleague.

To take this example one final step, it's possible that someone in these officers' earlier lives had been critical of them, or perhaps even bullying toward them. They both perceived the presence of criticism and bullying in their environment when it wasn't there, and then behaved in exactly that way – critical and bullying – in response to my challenge. It was what they knew. They had been taught to behave in this way by their childhood models, while I struggled to override my perfectionism and instinct to play by the rules – something I'd learned from mine.

> What I can say is that I've never experienced
> another situation quite like that again,
> because I was able to reflect on it and
> understand what had happened.

Now, with the benefit of time, I can hold those officers' probable early experience gently and compassionately in my mind, knowing that it was never really about me anyway – in the same way that my perfectionism was nothing to do with them.

Relational Trauma

Relational trauma, as we've previously discussed, is the type of trauma that occurs within the attachment relationship itself. Rather than being the result of a one-off accident or a natural disaster, relational trauma happens during the delicate dance of being in relationship with another human being.

> There are so many people for whom
> relational trauma has had an impact.

However, because it is often less extreme, it can be difficult to pinpoint what caused it or what it originally looked like.

The lack of awareness around this type of trauma is one of the biggest challenges I've had to overcome as a therapist working with those who have experienced it. Many will argue that the types of interactions we might label as relational trauma are simply normal family dynamics, and it's for this reason that relational trauma can often go unrecognized for years. I believe that most of us have experienced a degree of this type of trauma, and the meaning that we take from these experiences becomes the driving force behind our thoughts, feelings, and behaviors for the rest of our lives, unless we seek to change things. For those of us with the courage to draw back the curtain, understanding relational trauma and what we experienced as children allows us to become better-functioning adults, parents, friends, and coworkers. It also allows us to understand the true core origins of the psychological difficulties that we experience. It's our yellow brick road, finally leading us to understand our struggles with anxiety, depression, and other psychological disorders or difficulties.

I once shared a post online about relational trauma. One angry commenter told me that I was pathologizing normal family interactions, and that this was not only unhelpful but irresponsible. This isn't an unusual reaction, but I think it tells its own story. Usually, strong reactions like this suggest that the content has triggered an awareness in that person that wasn't present before. That can be jarring and I do understand. I wonder if this resonates with you, too.

> Often, it can feel quite triggering to surrender to the knowledge that what came before for us wasn't actually OK.

One of the biggest reasons that people struggle to acknowledge a degree of relational trauma is that they perhaps also had parents who were at times loving and supportive. We worry that we're blaming the people in our lives who, despite their flaws, loved and looked after us. But this doesn't have to be an 'either... or' situation. It can be a 'both... and,' in which we can say, for the most part, that our parents loved us and did what they could with the knowledge, access to resources, and level of self-awareness that they had at the time, while modeling some unhelpful behaviors and patterns, too.

BETH'S STORY

Beth came to me looking to understand her challenges with her mental health and her relationship with her mother. She had begun following me after she had seen one of my social media posts on relational trauma that had resonated with her. Beth was aware that her childhood conditioning meant that she struggled to speak up for herself and hold boundaries with others. She also had problems with anxiety and reported the physical manifestations of the stress she felt, with chronic stomach pains being a recurring problem for her.

Beth had been born in the north of England. When she was around four or five, the family moved to Aberdeen, Scotland, where they remained for several years. Beth had one sister and her mum looked after them at home while her father worked. After a few years, Beth's mother wanted to move back to England to be closer to her family support networks. This meant that by the age of eight, Beth had attended three primary schools and was, in her own words, 'always the new girl.' She acknowledged how deeply this had affected her confidence.

When the family moved back to England, Beth's father set himself up in business. Unfortunately, the business later failed, and Beth's mother was forced to go back to work. Beth recalled that her mother would frequently talk of being picked on and bullied in the workplace. As an adult, Beth was now curious about her mother's frequent relational difficulties and wondered whether they occurred in response to how her mother treated her colleagues.

In high school, Beth initially found it very tough to make friends. Reflecting as an adult on that time, she said that she thought she was experiencing relationship difficulties herself and she had no memory of anyone in her life validating her emotional experience at that time. She eventually made friends with a group of girls, but also recognized that they were all in need of support. She herself was perceived by others as 'geeky' as she had done very well in her exams. Beth acknowledged seeking validation and approval through her academic abilities. After high school, Beth was told she couldn't move out to attend university as money was very tight for the family.

Eventually, around the age of 21, she moved in with her sister, who she then discovered drank and took drugs recreationally. When she questioned her sister's behavior, she was accused of being 'no fun' and told she was 'boring.' Beth described feeling 'very alone' as a consequence of her living situation. She felt then, and said she still felt now, the sadness of having no lifelong friends and struggling with family relationships.

Beth's parents split acrimoniously when she was in her twenties. She pointed out that her mother frequently talked of the narcissistic abuse she had endured at the hands of her father. However, Beth's own perception of her parents' relationship was very different from that of her mother. The narrative around this from her mother didn't feel correct to Beth, with her mother frequently taking on a victim role in a similar way to how she had described being victimized in the workplace.

Later, Beth struggled in her own romantic relationships and in one relationship she acknowledged she had made a particularly poor choice of partner. Though he was a good person, she hadn't been able to envisage a future with this man. However, he had been 'approved of' by her mother. This meant that she'd perhaps stayed in this relationship longer than she might have.

The impact of her early life experiences and her ongoing family dynamics was evident. Though Beth was an incredibly smart and capable woman, she struggled with her confidence and felt that everybody was lying to her or out to get her. She was fearful of her current partner leaving her and felt ashamed of how she felt about this, too. In schema therapy, which you will hear more about soon, these specific challenges align with a 'mistrust/abuse' schema or relational pattern, where core beliefs might include 'people can't be trusted' or 'people will hurt me,' and also an 'abandonment' schema, in which we might hold an assumption that those that we love will leave us one day. Beth clearly felt abandoned by her parents as a child emotionally and anything she did now as an adult was judged by them, too. She was controlled by her mother's views and opinions, and had got to a point in her life where she recognized how this was impacting her negatively. She subjugated her own needs to please others. Subjugation is another schema or pattern that we can pick up in relation to our childhood conditioning.

At the time we worked together, Beth felt that no matter what she did, her mother had a knack of making her feel bad or guilty about it. More recently, she had started to question her mother over the unkind or judgmental things she said to her and her behavior toward her. Calling her out felt challenging, as it went against all the conditioning of her childhood and clearly distinguished her from her sister, who chose to ignore their mother's behavior instead. The discomfort that this created left Beth feeling dysregulated and uncomfortable.

As Beth got stronger and challenged her mother's judgments and control more, her mother didn't react well. Beth wondered if it was in fact her mother who demonstrated narcissistic traits and who lacked insight into her own behavior. Beth was now a mother herself, and her children's relationship to their grandmother and how they were impacted by her behavior was one of the reasons she'd decided to address things. Her children had begun to pick up on things that were being said to her and she knew the importance of modeling what she would and wouldn't accept and tolerate in relation to her own children's emotional development.

Beth was a working mother with a responsible professional job, but was often told by her mother that she should be home 'looking after her children,' which is of course what her mother herself had done. What her mother didn't expect was that Beth's way of looking after her children involved limiting their contact with their grandmother to reduce any harm caused by her. Beth worried that her response was harsh, but she knew that it would give her time to develop her ongoing strategy for minimizing the impact that contact with her mother had. This work also helped Beth to understand that though it might feel difficult to hold these boundaries, it was also necessary, at least for a time.

When Beth had similar conversations with her father, he reacted very differently. In contrast, he had apologized and accepted the difficulties present in Beth's childhood. This validation of how Beth had experienced her childhood went some way to begin to address the dearth of emotional support she had received back then.

Looking through the lens of relational trauma, Beth was able to see where her past, and particularly her relationship with her mother, had caused her to relate to herself and others in predictable but sometimes unhelpful ways. Having recently been offered a promotion at work, she noticed how her confidence and holding boundaries with others could be difficult for her. This is how her trauma showed up in her today. Beth was invested in doing the inner work needed to address this and though her relationship with her mum remains challenging, she knows that anything is possible when she does this work and continues to meet her own needs unapologetically.

Who Do You Think You Are?

Separate from attachment in the traditional sense, there's a type of attachment that I want to highlight as we conclude this chapter. Though I've largely outlined my clinical understanding of attachment, childhood conditioning, and trauma, anecdotally I've also noticed that we can become attached to who we 'believe' we are. Sometimes, it's the strength of this particular belief that can keep us stuck for years. We've been fed a narrative, projected on to us from our parents, of who we are, what we like, and what we stand for. We believe it, because the adults who loved us told us so. These beliefs can often set the tone for our lives. The good news is you get to put pen to paper and rewrite that narrative for yourself.

WHAT HAVE YOU LEARNED?

Take some time to consider the following points and write out your answers in your journal. This will help prepare you for putting together your own psychological formulation later in this book.

1. After reading this chapter, what have you come to understand differently about your own attachment relationships and childhood conditioning?

2. What is your perspective on trauma now? Has trauma been a part of your life?

3. Is there anything else you have realized about your own childhood experiences or life experiences that give you some clues as to how you might need to address or change things for the future?

CHAPTER 5

Digging Deeper

In the world of talking therapies, cognitive behavioral therapy (CBT) is integral to delivering quality treatment for those struggling psychologically. It's the foundation upon which many other therapies are built, and was developed by the American psychiatrist Aaron T. Beck and his daughter Judith S. Beck in 1994. CBT's basic premise is that our thoughts, feelings, and behaviors are interlinked, and that if we can address unhelpful or negative thoughts then we can impact how we feel mentally and how we subsequently behave. Though many people will be familiar with the term 'CBT' or even with the therapy itself, I think that some may misunderstand what CBT can treat successfully and where it simply doesn't meet the brief, or falls short for some – and that could include you.

There is a basic assumption in CBT that it's our perception of an event in our life, rather than the event itself, that is most important in determining our individual thoughts, feelings, and reactions to it. A classic example of this might be getting ready to meet a friend for coffee. You've been looking forward to it all week. At the last minute, the friend cancels, saying she isn't feeling well. Now let's split you into Person A and Person B, to illustrate the different ways you might respond to that cancellation...

Person A says to themselves, 'What a shame, I hope they feel better soon and we can rearrange for next weekend' (thought). They feel disappointed, but know there'll be another coffee meet-up soon (feeling). They text their friend back and wish them a speedy recovery (behavior). In contrast, Person B says to themselves, 'Not again, they're always cancelling on me. Maybe they just don't want to spend time with me anymore because I'm too needy' (thought). They feel let down, hurt, and embarrassed (feeling). They don't respond for a few days and when they do, they minimize what happened and don't enquire about their friend's health, as they remain too distracted by their own emotions (behavior). The example highlights how the same event can be perceived and reacted to completely differently by two people. It's their unique and individual perspective on the event that changes both how they feel and their subsequent behavior.

A traditional CBT approach would look to identify the 'thinking error' present in Person B's response – in this case, mind-reading (believing you know what another person is thinking) and catastrophizing (thinking the worst). The trouble with this approach is that even if we know that the way Person B thinks about this event is because they've been let down their entire life and told they were 'too needy,' CBT usually has less scope to address this. The treatment is focused more on the cognitive reframe and the individual rather than the relational. This means that in CBT we are often examining our thinking and seeking to address the underlying thinking style, rather than the experiential factors from our past that perhaps led us down the route toward thinking this way in the first place.

While in my clinical practice, for example, I've used the basic principles of CBT to engage therapeutically with many people,

I'm also aware that it neglects the underpinning relational experiences that have caused the person to respond in a particular way. This can often be because in CBT we're usually quite focused on engaging at the thought level and symptom reduction, rather than always delving deeper. CBT incorporates collaboration with the client to ensure shared goals for treatment. An expectation is also set around active participation on the part of the client, and ongoing monitoring of change. CBT also requires the building of a sound therapeutic relationship, from within which meaningful change can be facilitated. This is done through offering the client genuine unconditional positive regard.

Intrinsic to all therapies, unconditional positive regard (UPR) was developed by Stanley Standal in 1954 and then popularized a couple of years later by the psychologist Carl Rogers, the founder of person-centered therapy. What UPR means in practice is meeting the client exactly where they are with empathy, nonjudgment, and compassion, no matter what they bring to the therapy space. CBT is also underpinned by some key components and concepts such as core beliefs and dysfunctional assumptions, which are important to know and understand. This is because our core beliefs and our 'go to' dysfunctional assumptions are often our instinctual knee-jerk reactions to the situations we might face in our here and now, and are typically unhelpful.

Core Beliefs

Core beliefs are those things that we believe wholeheartedly to be true about ourselves, others, and the world around us, even in the face of evidence to the contrary. These beliefs impact how we perceive events and show up in the world. Using the earlier example, Person B's core beliefs might sound something like, 'I'm too much/needy,' and, 'Other people will let me down.' Core beliefs can be difficult to shift, but with time and commitment, it's possible to change.

Dysfunctional Assumptions

Dysfunctional assumptions are like the rules we live by that are automatic responses to events in our life. They are often expressed as 'if… then' statements and arise out of the core beliefs and schemas (patterns of relating) we've developed through our experiences. An example for Person B might be, 'If people let me down, then I'm worthless.'

Negative Automatic Thoughts and Thinking Errors

Negative automatic thoughts are the thoughts we think in relation to life events. They are often irrational, self-critical, and in line with the core beliefs that we have developed. Thinking errors are very specific errors in our thinking that shape our behavioral response. Common thinking errors, also known as distortions, might include personalizing (when we assume responsibility for things that aren't really anything to do with us or our fault) or blaming others for how you feel.

What's the Evidence?

Now, I want to make my position on this clear. CBT is fundamental to psychological work. For many psychological disorders, there is a strong evidence base for CBT as a treatment approach. Difficulties like panic disorder, social anxiety, and obsessive compulsive disorder (OCD) are just some of the issues for which a CBT approach is officially recommended.

As a clinical psychologist in Scotland, when considering which treatment approach or therapy to use, I would typically consult a document called the 'Matrix', which is pulled together by senior clinicians and the Scottish Government. It's a comprehensive guide that outlines the current evidence base and best treatment approach for psychological difficulties and disorder, depending on severity. Anyone can look at the Matrix online (see www.matrix.nhs.scot). In addition to reviewing it, I would encourage you to educate yourself by doing a little research of your own into the sorts of evidence-based treatments that are available and recommended in your part of the world.

However, despite the evidence base, for the clients and services I worked with, CBT alone didn't always seem to offer a comprehensive solution. It's often felt like only one piece of a much more complicated jigsaw puzzle and I know many people struggling with their psychological well-being may feel like this, too.

MEGHAN'S STORY

Meghan came to me shortly after her twin girls started going to school, which she felt had brought to mind past events of her own that she still needed to process. She described feeling down, overwhelmed with life, and wanting to be more in control. She noted that she found it very difficult to be present and 'in the moment,' and recognized that she had an overactive brain and racing thoughts. A few months prior to engaging in therapy, Meghan's mood had become very low, and she had decided to take some time off work to prioritize her mental health. Describing herself as a shell of her former self, Meghan felt physically exhausted, was experiencing heightened emotions, and was often tearful at home and during our sessions. She also acknowledged feeling alone in her struggles despite her husband being largely supportive. Meghan wanted support now to improve her mood, feel more in control, and process some of what she had experienced through the birth of her twins. She also indicated that she'd seen a psychologist as a child, which was linked to past events. She seemed unsure of the relatedness of this to her current situation.

Taking me back to when she had given birth to her girls, Meghan described it as a lonely time. Though the pregnancy had been planned, having two babies was unexpected, and Meghan remembered feeling overwhelmed at first by the news that she was expecting twins. As is often the case when people announce they're having twins, Meghan's family and friends were delighted. However, Meghan was worried about the financial costs and care implications of two babies, and felt sad for what might have been for just one baby, who would have had her undivided attention. However, she didn't talk about those feelings as she felt guilty about them. The girls were later born prematurely, requiring treatment within the special care baby unit and various interventions, including for their lung development.

Today, Meghan realized that five years on from welcoming her babies into the world, the shock of learning she was having twins, the trauma of the birth itself, and a number of subsequent emergency medical events involving the girls had finally caught up with her. Meghan's fear that her babies could die had never left her and she was hypervigilant to any perceived threats within her environment that could harm her children. She felt depressed and her symptoms were largely consistent with that picture. She also admitted to having flashbacks when she became particularly anxious, and together we identified a strong core belief that she herself was 'not loveable.'

When considering low mood and depression, one of the first-line treatments for an initial episode of mild to moderate depression is CBT. Other indicated interventions include guided self-help, behavioral activation, or IPT (interpersonal psychotherapy), depending on the intensity of intervention required. However, in Meghan's case there were also symptoms indicative of a possible post-traumatic response. What I became particularly curious about was when her core belief of feeling unlovable had developed. This didn't seem to fit with the overall picture, and it was important to assess Meghan further to understand more about her earlier past and determine whether CBT would meet the brief or whether something else might be required by way of intervention.

Session by session, I gently began to uncover Meghan's developmental history. Meghan acknowledged that her mum and dad had separated when she was young and that she hadn't coped well with this change in her family life. Through exploration, she told me how she'd felt abandoned by her dad, from whom she was now estranged as an adult, although her brother remained in contact with him. Meghan explained how her mum had also struggled with the split and had never been able to open up to anyone or deal with the fallout from it. Consequently, Meghan learned from her mother how to push away and suppress emotions.

When I asked Meghan what else her mother had taught her, she told me two things. Firstly, that she had instilled in her how important it was to work hard and, secondly, that it was not OK to feel her emotions. Meghan had been angry with her mum after the split and as an adult could see how she blamed her mum and took out her frustration both on her and on herself in the form of self-harming and occasional violent outbursts. This is what had prompted her work with a psychologist previously.

It became clear that one of the core difficulties Meghan needed to address was how challenging she found it to communicate her true feelings. Though CBT formed the basic beginnings of our work, more was needed to address the deeper relational issues and attachment difficulties exacerbated by the family separation. Her reaction to her birth trauma was not something that reframing unhelpful cognitions would shift alone. As well as doing trauma-processing work related to her experiences in hospital, Meghan needed to understand the underpinning mechanism of how her own parental attachment disruption, through her dad leaving and the subsequent negative impact on her mum's parenting, had left a wound that she had been taught to avoid and pretend wasn't there.

What seemed clear was that the birth of her babies had activated a strong maternal instinct in Meghan. She wanted to protect them. But more than that – the trauma of their birth and subsequent events had uncovered the previously buried trauma from Meghan's own childhood and the source of her core belief that she was unlovable. I've heard similar versions of this from many mothers: That giving birth is often experienced as traumatic, and that the experience itself of becoming a parent and the strong feelings this evokes then offers a new perspective on your own childhood.

Meghan found it hard to understand how her parents had related to her and how she now sought to relate to her own girls positively. Over the course of our work together, she became better able to communicate her feelings to her closest family. She was, for example, able to talk with her mum about the past in order to learn more about how her mum had attempted to cope with it. She was also able to discuss things more openly with her husband, which meant she felt more connected and less alone.

Meghan needed that relational slant in therapy to make sense of it all. Over time, she began to feel more joyful as a parent, rather than crippled with the fear that something terrible might happen to her girls. After our work together ended, Meghan contacted me one day out of the blue to say that life had transformed for her. She was back to work, feeling more in control, and spending time with her family at a caravan by the sea. Proof, I think, of the importance of slowing down and prioritizing ourselves when life catches up with us.

Clinical Training and CBT

During my doctoral training at the University of Edinburgh, the model that was intrinsic to our training was CBT. As trainees, we were assessed by how well we aligned ourselves with the CBT principles and approach in our one-to-one sessions with patients. Sometimes we would be observed in clinic by our supervisors, who would be present in the room with us. At other times, we would take a recording of the session and it would be assessed against a checklist of what was typically expected in a session from a CBT perspective.

Now, while this was all necessary and helpful in honing our therapeutic skills, often, both in training and in my professional life after qualification, it was evident that something more than CBT was required. This depended on so many factors, including the patient themselves, the type of presenting problem, the setting, or circumstances.

Ultimately, when something feels so
structured and prescriptive, it perhaps
misses the mark or the nuance of things.

As my clinical training was coming to a close, there was a move toward opening up the models we were trained in and incorporating an additional core model of therapy. This was welcomed across the board and I chose cognitive analytical therapy (CAT). It was a model underpinned by CBT, but which also had a strong relational component based in reciprocity and attachment. It was a good fit for the types of clients I worked with, and I loved having a broader relational scope from within which to work with people.

One of the most helpful elements of CAT involved 'mapping' relationships and understanding how and why we would develop certain ways of relating to our self and others. This 'relational mapping,' as I've termed it, can be entirely transformative in therapy, because it very quickly gets to the nub of the problem, and then identifies how to exit the unhelpful relational patterns and cycles that we can find ourselves in. Later in this book, you'll be asked to complete relational maps corresponding to the influential people in your life.

CBT *in Practice*

After six years of hard work, a wedding day, a pregnancy, and the birth of my daughter during my doctoral training years, I qualified as a clinical psychologist. In my practice post-qualification, I could see even more clearly the gaps that CBT did not fill. More recently in my private practice, and through sharing my views on social media, I've had many people tell me that CBT simply didn't work for them.

I've seen time and time again how people would perhaps have been offered CBT for anxiety or low mood in alignment with the latest evidence base. For some people, the course of treatment would work. Their symptoms of anxiety, low mood, or their phobia would be reduced to acceptable levels and they would continue about their lives, utilizing the strategies they had been taught regularly or just when they needed to. For others, their symptoms would improve for a short time and then return perhaps six months later. I've heard countless stories of how, for some, they experienced a revolving door of cyclical periods of poor mental health and treatment that didn't work.

> Anecdotally, I've found that when you scratch the surface of these people's stories, there exists a degree of trauma that has never been uncovered before, far less addressed.

The issues central to why the problem arose in the first place have not been processed fully within the scope that CBT allows. The other issue I know many people have with CBT is the idea that it's simply their thinking that is faulty. Indeed, some of the language used within CBT – such as 'thinking errors' – leans toward that. It individualizes the problem somewhat and suggests that there is something intrinsically wrong with the way that you think, rather than identifying and focusing on where this type of thinking might have arisen due to your experiences.

Personally, I thought and felt all sorts of things in the immediate aftermath of Matty's death. A few examples stick out. The first was the morning Matty died. Several hours later, after being asked to give a statement to the police, I was sitting on my bed with one of my best friends. We were quietly talking through what the police had asked and trying to make sense of what had been said. I was very clearly shell-shocked. (Incidentally, the term 'shell-shocked' comes from the reaction of soldiers in World War I, who'd been traumatized by what they'd seen and developed symptoms of post-traumatic stress disorder (PTSD). It refers to the mental confusion and upset that we experience after traumatic events.)

Suddenly, through the fog of this mental confusion, I realized what Matty's death meant for me. My children had been my first thought in the hospital. Now, sat on the edge of the bed, the same bed that we had slept together in just hours before, I asked my friend for reassurance that I was right about it. 'So, I'm a widow now?' I asked. She nodded and my head fell, my chin soaked by tears that had trickled down my face and onto my constricted throat.

The clarity in my confusion felt like both a relief and a life sentence. So many thoughts flooded my mind: 'I'll be alone for the rest of my life' and 'I won't be able to cope with this.' Were these thoughts a knee-jerk reaction? Yes. Were they rational? Of course not. But it wouldn't have been appropriate in that moment to deny or invalidate my natural emotional response by trying to reframe my thoughts to 'you'll have friends and family to lean on for support,' and 'you'll meet someone when and if ever you're ready.' It would have been too early for any of that. However, had these thoughts persisted for a longer period of time, then a reframe might have been more helpful and appropriate. In the end, I got exactly what I needed several months later, when I went to see another clinical psychologist who had lost a spouse. And it was not CBT.

I'd known this psychologist through my clinical training as my out-of-area mentor. Aware that he'd lost his wife, I sought him out now. When I saw him for a couple of sessions in that first year after Matty's death, I was strangely comforted that he lived in a familiar little village, right next to the University of Stirling, where I had studied for my first psychology degree years before. I looked forward to that drive, in which I often fantasized that I was simply going back to university after the weekend. I imagined that I still had all of my life choices to come, no dead husband, and that my children had not been bereaved. I also remember my internal dialogue and vowing not to cry or come across as 'not coping' in the session – further evidence of my emotional suppression. But once inside the safety of the therapy space, I simply couldn't contain my grief and anguish.

Looking back, I was all over the place, parenting three grieving children, and I struggled with the commitment of therapy over the longer term. But despite my chaotic presentation (the way I appeared and behaved in the sessions), my therapist seemed to know exactly what I needed. As I broke down in his beautiful living room, with its comfortable upholstered chairs and high bay windows, he paused, took a breath, and told me, 'I'm OK now. I've met someone and I'm happy. You will be, too, one day.' His words meant everything to me. It was enough. I am so grateful for his skill in picking up on the relational attachment basis of my pain.

I believed that being widowed meant I would never again feel truly happy – a negative and automatic assumption. He knew intuitively what I needed to hear. He cut through my irrational thinking and bypassed the surface level of my presentation to get to the deeper relational meaning for me. He recognized my fear of not coping and losing control. He called it out gently by using himself as the vehicle, validated and reassured me, and from that place I was able to both heal and grow. As I write this, I'm crying for that version of me who felt so alone and hopeless, and also in gratitude for that moment in therapy that helped to turn things around.

A Relational Problem Requires a Relational Solution

So, what are we to do when CBT is not what's required? Well, I was lucky enough to work in the types of services throughout my career in which the degree of complexity in people's presentations meant that I was able to train in and utilize additional therapeutic models. These models got to the core of the difficulties, which were usually relational and attachment-based.

> When we have relational difficulties, it seems intuitive to me that we require a relational-level solution.

Though CBT does seek to formulate and tell the story of why the person is presenting with this problem at this time, and that might incorporate a relational understanding of the problem, the treatment itself doesn't necessarily allow for a truly relational focus, remaining mostly at the thought level. Consider, for a moment, Beth's experience through a CBT lens. Her presenting problem was anxiety. CBT is likely to have pointed out that her anxiety was driven solely by her thoughts and potentially sought to reframe or restructure them. And though the CBT formulation would have acknowledged her relationship with her mother and its impact on her core beliefs, its scope to treat the significant, underlying relational problems would have been limited.

Reciprocity

In relational approaches to therapeutic work, reciprocity is the focus. We help people to understand how crucial relationships have been to their emotional development, and how they will continue to be so for them in the future. Reciprocity is a core component of dialectical behavioral therapy, known as DBT. Founded by the psychologist Marsha Linehan in the late 1970s, DBT is typically used for those who struggle with emotional regulation, among other challenges.

> Reciprocity itself involves a sense of equality, cooperation, and mutual exchange within our relationships. If we didn't have that when we were growing up, the goal is to cultivate it.

In DBT, the relationship we build in therapy is the vehicle. Reciprocity involves healthy attachment without codependence. In our daily lives, this means being able to engage in a relationship with someone, while also cultivating outside interests and relationships with others. In cognitive analytic therapy, too, reciprocity is believed to form an important part in raising people's awareness. In CAT, one of the building blocks is called the reciprocal role procedure, or RRP. I usually refer to it as simply the relationship.

I'm now going to walk you through how I would explain the RRP and its importance within the therapy space. My aim here is to simplify the terminology and allow you to apply the theory to yourself in the next part of the book. The other thing to know about CAT, and why I love it as an approach, is that the words we use as descriptors within the therapeutic process matter. They must resonate with your own experience, and in that way the RRP becomes individually tailored. Ultimately, it gives that all-important sense of being truly heard and validated when words are used that are meaningful to you. For me, as a writer and a lover of words, what could be better!

The Reciprocal Relationship

First, we need to go back to attachment. Now, in any relationship we must, of course, have two people who exist in relation to one another. In CAT, the RRP model depicts this relationship with one person in the top pole or position, and the other person in the bottom pole or position. There is nothing intrinsically good or bad about either the top or bottom position.

Now, in the attachment relationship, imagine the parent/caregiver assumes the top pole and the child the bottom pole. Ideally, we're hoping that during the attachment process, the parent is loving and supportive, for example. If they are, the child, who has assumed the bottom pole, learns what it feels like to be loved and supported. In addition to having a felt sense of love and support, they are also modeled to by the adult what it is to be loving and supportive. Remember, social modeling theory says that our parents or caregivers show us certain behaviors, which we then observe and copy. In this way, we learn both the feelings and the behaviors associated with love and support, and can take these and the learned relational pattern into our adult lives. Crucially, we can then show love and support to ourselves and others.

But what if our experience wasn't loving and supportive? Or what if, alongside love and support, there were also high levels of control or criticism? Well, this time the critical and controlling adult is modeling this behavior to a criticized and controlled child. The difference in this scenario is that it's not a positive experience. The child has a felt sense of being controlled and criticized, which can feel emotionally intolerable to them. In response, they might seek to escape the cycle and the associated negative feelings. They could do this by adapting their behavior to reduce the likelihood of criticism by acquiescing to the parent's needs, wants, and desires. Or, and this is where it gets truly fascinating to me, they might 'flip' from the bottom pole and try to adopt the top one. This is more likely in adulthood, of course, when the individual has more scope to do so.

Let me explain that further. Remember, the child is also modeled to by the parent, and if the parent is critical and controlling, the child learns how to behave in that way. This reciprocal relational pattern becomes part of the child's emotional repertoire and is taken with them into adult life. This can mean that when, as an adult, they feel controlled or criticized in some way, they may try to escape the cycle by, for example, people-pleasing. Alternatively, they may try to adopt the top position by becoming controlling or critical toward the other. Sometimes, they may feel like they are fluctuating between the two poles, before doing an eventual 180-degree flip. They learned the pattern after all.

Still with me? OK. One final point on this. The relational patterns that we learn can be applied in our relationship with our self, others, and often with both.

We can both internalize and externalize these unhelpful patterns.

What that might look like in our example is that the child who is on the receiving end of controlling or critical behavior from their adult caregiver might grow up to be highly critical of themselves and others as an adult.

In therapy, I've used this relational mapping process, facilitated by the RRP model from Ryle and Kerr (2002) to get to the core of the person's relational difficulties, usually relatively quickly. If a person is triggered by feeling criticized or controlled, as in the above example, the chances are they've been in a position before of feeling that way. This gives us a starting point to work back from. We can begin to examine their childhood conditioning in more detail, asking questions that elicit the detail and nuance of the key relationships in their life.

In Part III of *What to Do When You Feel Broken*, we will start to pull together all the learning from the first two sections of the book so that you can start to self-formulate your unique psychological story, and relational mapping will be a part of that, too.

Relational Patterns and Time

It's important to note here that across our psychological development, and through our lifetime, we develop many relational patterns that we add to and select from our repertoire when interacting with others. In doing the psychological work in this book, we are attempting to develop an awareness of the patterns that are unhealthy or unhelpful, and reduce our reliance on them as our 'go to' ways of behaving. At the same time, we are hoping to strengthen the healthy relational patterns we have and emphasize their use over the unhealthy ones.

This is not a process that can occur overnight, so I'd like to manage your expectations around this.

> Too often, self-development and psychological work are sold as a quick fix. I understand the desire to promise quick results, but this can often set people up to fail.

As a clinical psychologist, I'm always looking for the gap where knowledge, awareness, and different behaviors can be cultivated. We need to challenge ourselves just enough that this moves the needle, while also giving us a sense of success or mastery. Otherwise, we simply give up. The relational patterns that you're beginning to become more aware of developed over many years; in fact, some of them could even be intergenerational, as we will explore in the next chapter. It's unrealistic to assume we can change them quickly. I want you to think of this work and the changes you wish to make as an ongoing process of assimilation.

WHAT HAVE YOU LEARNED?

Take some time to consider the following points and write out your answers in your journal. This will help prepare you for putting together your own psychological formulation later in this book.

1. After reading this chapter, what are your general reflections?

2. Do you have a sense of particular unhelpful core beliefs that you live with?

3. Can you identify any common dysfunctional assumptions or negative automatic thoughts that limit you?

4. What sense do you have of whether the challenges you face might have their origins in your early relationships?

CHAPTER 6

Intergenerational Trauma

In addition to recognizing the relational trauma that we may have experienced throughout our own childhoods, if we're truly to understand ourselves and where our patterns originated and formed, we have to be aware of the intergenerational nature of trauma. Past trauma is relational too and the experiences of our family will have shaped up their own world views, how they feel about themselves and others, and how they subsequently parent, model behaviors, and respond to us. There is a relational kick down the generational line that is behavioral in nature.

But what about genetics? Well, we are now learning more and more about the biological nature of trauma, and how the experiences of trauma transcend the relational and become part of the very fabric of what we pass on to our children. Our trauma is literally stored within our DNA or genetic coding. This is the mechanism by which intergenerational trauma, experienced by our family of origin, can also be passed down the genetic line. Those experiencing intergenerational trauma may be subject to the symptoms, responses, patterns, and psychological effects from the trauma their family members went through years before.

These findings are so important. Firstly, because they offer further nuance to our understanding of how trauma works. Secondly, I believe that when we can acknowledge the part-biological basis of trauma, this reduces the blame that we often apportion to others or assign to ourselves. It offers a chance for compassion in the face of adversity and to take responsibility for what is ours – and to reject what is not.

Three Generations

Nan was born in a small village known locally as the Roman Camps in 1931. Situated near Edinburgh in Scotland, 'the camps' was a small collection of houses on the outskirts of a much larger town. The houses there had been allocated to the foremen and workers of the local shale mine, and it was a thriving community within a community. The mine extracted shale oil from the land to make paraffin by-products.

Nan was an only child, her father was a storeman at the mine and her mother a housewife who had been in service prior to her marriage. A former solider, Nan's father had lost an arm in World War One. Nan and he were close and when he died, she was badly affected by his loss. She grew up in a time when families supported each other, lived close by, and where her maternal cousins and extended family were incredibly important for community and survival. She married at the age of 21 and had her first baby at 24. That baby was my mum and Nan is my grandmother.

My experience of Nan was of a warm and loving woman who also had high expectations of how we were supposed to look and behave. I remember bath time at her house when I went for sleepovers. She would scrub my scalp, nails up, to make sure I was clean. But she always had a warm fluffy towel hanging on the radiator to dry my brother and me with afterward. Then we would sit cozy on the couch with hot 'roasted cheese' made in the grill with thick slices of bread, watching *The Golden Girls* on TV.

She was like that with most things. A bit of a contradiction. A scratched scalp before a soft towel. Controlling commands, driven largely by anxiety, before a comforting bowl of tattie soup. There was a right way and a wrong way to do things, and love and affection was shown through actions rather than words or touch. She was also an incredibly kind soul, and would visit and support others less fortunate than herself. She could, and frequently would, strike up conversations with strangers on the street.

Often, she took my brother Dave and me on bus trips into Edinburgh, where we would wander round Jenners, a large department store, before going for strawberry milkshakes and salty chips at McDonald's on Princes Street. I have multiple recollections of times when, on these occasions, she seemed compelled to point out a disabled child or a homeless person in the street who she perceived as being less fortunate than we were ourselves. She would tell us, far too loudly for my comfort, 'how lucky we were' not to be in that position. Though I understood the intention behind it was to promote gratitude, the result of this for me was a sense of shame or embarrassment at my able body and warm bed to go home to. I knew I didn't like that feeling and I remember trying to avoid these exchanges.

I didn't really notice the impact of this until years later, when I was allocated a clinical training place within the incredibly niche field of forensic learning disabilities. This concerned those people who had been born with cognitive deficits and had later committed offences. When I got the training place, I was of course delighted, but felt worried about how working in this area for five years would feel. In the end, I think it was a serendipitous twist of fate and an opportunity to heal an aspect of my own psychosocial development that had limited me in ways I'd been unaware of before then. The shame I'd experienced in those moments with my gran had induced either an avoidance or an overcompensation, depending on the situation or how you found me. I was therefore able to engage fully with the issues and to shift my unhelpful coping strategies over time.

But what was it about my gran's own psychological development that had compelled her to seek out the less fortunate and make reparations by acknowledging their lack of privilege, able body, or some other perceived limitation? Despite being from a working-class background, did she have a sense of the privilege she enjoyed and did she feel shame? Had her father losing an arm in the war influenced her attitude toward those with physical disabilities? We can never know for sure, as I can't ask her those questions now. After living for a while with dementia, she died in 2018, just six months before my husband. It's an awful irony that I sat at her funeral, Matty squeezing my hand, as I said my tearful goodbye to her, not knowing that the next funeral I'd attend would be his.

Though from a working-class background, 'Granny Mac,' as we referred to her, was employed as a personal assistant in the office of the Lord Lyon King of Arms of Scotland. The Lord Lyon was responsible for determining what was appropriate for inclusion on coats of arms, as the visual designs placed on a shield or tabard in Scotland are meant to represent the story of an individual, family, or organization. Prior to this, she had worked in a lawyer's office. She took her roles seriously, was a hard worker, and it would be fair to say she also believed herself to be important, even inside of a class structure above her own. She had what seemed to me to be an unshakeable sense of self, was aware of her striking looks, loved social interaction, yet despite all that she was an anxious worrier.

My grandfather, on the other hand, appeared quite shy and could be socially avoidant. Like many, he would lubricate himself with alcohol and would then become the life and soul of any gathering or party. My grandad had grown up in a family with five siblings. He had become an upholsterer and despite being an intelligent and well-read man, my grandfather's sense of self rested on less solid ground. He had been medically retired in his early fifties. He could almost be described as most comfortable when solitary and had a tendency, I would say, toward low mood. In his own way, he was also loving and kind, and often slipped a £10-note secretly into your hand as you left the house.

His introversion and my grandmother's extroversion were an interesting juxtaposition to parent from. While in his later years my grandfather would sit at home, read, watch documentaries, and obliterate crosswords with his extensive vocabulary, my grandmother, by contrast, was 'never off the top of the road,' as we say in Scotland. She was active, engaged socially, and a low mood never seemed to darken her door. Though I wonder now how much of this was masking, which is when someone attempts to camouflage their real feelings in order to blend in and be seen as acceptable to others.

Into this marriage my own mother was born. She grew up with a similar sense of family and community around her on both sides. Born at home in the same village where my gran had lived as a girl, she was an only child until the age of 11. Often looked after by her maternal grandmother, my mum is intelligent, infinitely capable, and can turn her hand to anything. She is, of course, the product of her own mother and father. They parented her with high expectations, introversion, extroversion, and a smattering of anxiety and depression that no one particularly spoke of. Some of this is of its time, of course. Mental health was not an accessible conversation in her early childhood or within the Scottish cultural landscape.

My mum's more natural tendency is toward introversion. All her life, she's shied away from any kind of spotlight or from taking up space. Despite this, she thrived in school and from an early age she wanted to do well. She was regularly top of her class, played by the rules, and did as she was told. She was the definitive good girl. As my mum and I began reflecting on her upbringing, she couldn't necessarily see clearly where her parents had pushed her in certain directions. However, it seemed that the messaging she received was implicit but clear.

Academic achievement and learning were important, and she understood that she was expected to play by the rules.

By the time she reached her final year of high school, she admitted, the earlier shine of schooling was beginning to fade for her. Whatever satisfaction doing well academically had offered her had slowly diminished. As a consequence, she felt, she didn't work as hard as she might have done, and could have achieved better grades had she done so. She could see that there were other things in life and was tired of studying.

At that age, my mum didn't really know what she wanted to do with her life, but nonetheless her grades were good enough for her to apply to read law at university. I was curious whether my mum thought it coincidental that she had applied to study law when her own mother worked in a law firm. Given her uncertainty about her future career, she at least felt it was possible that she had done so to please her family. What was evident to my mum was that she knew soon after beginning her degree that she wasn't well suited to it. Away from the safety and security of home, she felt vulnerable.

While growing up, my mum acknowledged, emotional expression was quite limited within her family home. Neither her mother nor her father would ever tell her how they felt emotionally, and comforting touch and affection were not the norm. There was no emotional language spoken to scaffold or contain feelings. This is when our caregivers help us manage our emotions well, firstly by acknowledging they are present and normal, and secondly by offering comfort and suggesting strategies that might help regulate them. In schema therapy terms, my mum had experienced a degree of emotional deprivation. And so, when she ran into problems at university, it was challenging for her to communicate how she felt openly, and to be heard and understood fully. There simply wasn't the language or the culture for it within her family.

At the end of her first year, she told her parents that she didn't want to continue with her studies. Though she had friends at university, she simply didn't enjoy the lifestyle and would come home every weekend. Perhaps not understanding the true impact of lectures and of living away from the security of home, they persuaded her to continue regardless. Unsurprisingly, she did as was expected of her and played by their rules. A few times, worried for my mum's welfare, my gran left her work and traveled by train to see her. But despite witnessing her unhappiness, nobody felt able to say, 'Enough now,' and give her the permission she needed to stop.

Finally, two years later and in a heightened state of anxiety, my mum could no longer face her life as it was. She came home for good, retreating from the world for nearly a year, and leaving her law degree behind with a sigh of a relief and a sense of failure not of her own making. Disconnected and sad, her parents were ill-equipped to help her as she struggled to shake her core beliefs of 'not being good enough' and believing she had let others down.

Though not suicidal, she said, she had lost all interest in life. Her thoughts were initially externalized. Despite feeling as low and dark as she perhaps ever had, her worry was about what her choice meant for others, and then consequently what they and the rest of the world would think of her. This is an unhealthy but common way to choose to engage with the world – living with a fear of what others will think of us. It was this same fear that drove my grandmother to present herself in a certain way and made my own mum shrink into the shadows in shame.

But what about me? Well, I can tell you it's both driven me toward achievement and putting myself into spaces with confidence, and made me cower in metaphorical corners, desperate to remain unseen. In this way, intergenerational and relational trauma has imprinted its rather confusing legacy onto me. I know I'm myself a contradiction when I feel introversion knocking on my door, yet am still out there in the world, trying to make my mark. I recognize the anxiety, occasional low mood, and my trying desperately to be a 'good girl' who does the right thing. I'm aware it's there and choose to engage compassionately with it.

As I look back over the years, and think of Granny Mac, I am struck by a thought. Wouldn't it be transformative if we all had our very own personal coat of arms? A visual and physical representation of who we are, denoting the intricacies of our family, and communicating what we've been through and how this has molded us. A complex map laid out on a heavy metal shield to protect us and explain our story to both ourselves and to others. I think my Granny Mac would have liked this idea.

After emerging from her hiatus, my mum vowed that she never wanted to feel so low again. She saw how hurtful it was for her family to witness her retreat from life and yet feel so powerless. With the passing of time, Mum has acknowledged how what she went through back then made her stronger and more resilient. She told me that had she been able to talk about her feelings, then perhaps she would have been able to reconnect with the world, and her situation resolved sooner. In the post-traumatic growth phase of her experience, my mum met my dad. Fighting feelings of not being good enough for him either, one day the tide turned when my mum began listening to the 'healthy adult' inside her more keenly (*for more about the healthy adult inside each of us, see page 127*).

My family's trauma has traveled a distance, largely unseen through the generations. Three generations of relational interactions and trauma patterns have culminated in this daughter and mother using psychological knowledge to call out what came before. Not to blame or shame my family, but to acknowledge and say proudly that what I came from shaped who I am today – the insidious pain and patterns from my grandmother's generation to my mother's, landing like a seed and taking root at my feet. I think I might have been the first to really see it growing there.

My trauma is at once relational, intergenerational, and collective. It has found me through my experiences and my family, my biology, and the society and culture in which I have been brought up. Though it is me and I am it, I don't let it define me. Across my 40 years, it has been expressed as perfectionism and thinly veiled criticism; control and expectation; and unrelenting standards of striving and achieving. It has pushed me toward this profession of mine, and I am grateful in turn for what my profession has asked of me in building self-awareness. It's a gift from the universe. My 'small t' trauma that existed within the context of big love. And the 'big T' trauma that uncovered it all – the loss of my husband.

The Biopsychosocial Model, Stress, and Trauma

In psychology, we use the biopsychosocial model proposed by George L. Engel to explain the nature of our psychological difficulties (Engel, 1977). With trauma, I always try to explore and understand it using this framework, too. Firstly, this framework takes into consideration the biological nature of trauma, corresponding to the intergenerational ways that it can be passed down the genetic line. This might be through a predisposition to certain psychological disorders, as well as maladaptive ways of coping. Secondly, it acknowledges the psychological nature of trauma and the way we have been shaped by our relationships with others and their own unique psychological makeup. Finally, it recognizes the social nature of trauma and the way in which the wider culture and the society in which we live may have played their part in our collective trauma. In this way, the biopsychosocial model offers an integrated way of looking at trauma holistically.

Another helpful model to consider in this respect is known as the diathesis-stress model. This model, outlined by American clinical psychologist Paul Meehl in the 1960s, was used to explain the emergence of schizophrenia. In short, when the diathesis-stress model came along, it disrupted the nature–nurture debate in psychology by explaining how underlying vulnerabilities (diathesis) can interact with the stress we experience, causing us to develop psychological disorders. Many things can cause these underlying vulnerabilities. They can be biological – for example, with variations in our genes predisposing us to some psychological disorders. They can also entail life events, like the loss of a parent. (This is hard for me to hear, of course, as I know that because of my children's experiences, they now carry with them a predisposition that lies beyond my control.) Additionally, social or situational factors such as personality traits or living in a household with a low income, or having a parent with a psychological disorder, can also predispose us to difficulties.

However, it's important to remember that protective factors can reduce the impact of our predispositions, and that psychopathology is not inevitable. The other aspect of this model – stress – can also be considered variable. Acute stress might stem from a particular event, as in my case with the loss of a spouse, or it can be more chronic, as in the daily challenges of an abusive relationship. This model suggests that psychological struggle and disorder only arise when both an underlying vulnerability and stressors coincide to create that disorder.

With respect to your own journey, I think it's important to consider these models in terms of the impact that different biological, psychological, and social factors may have had on you. These factors will be very relevant when you are formulating your individual story later on in this book. For example, are you aware of any family members who've struggled with their mental health and who may have passed on these biological vulnerabilities? Are there any particular psychological factors such as personality traits that you're aware of, or that you may have been exposed to while growing up? Have there been any social factors or particular circumstances that may have shaped you, such as poverty or a significant life event, for example? What I want for you to reflect on is how these factors could have contributed to your feelings of brokenness. What part could they have played in your development and how your life is currently?

The Body and the Mind

Trauma has a way of making us singularly focused and hypervigilant. Healing asks us to pan out again and look at the wider picture.

In the days after my husband died, I was barely able to function. I wasn't sleeping, delaying lights out until the last possible moment, yet knowing I would be up at 5 a.m. with my twin boys. I didn't eat properly for at least two weeks and by the time Matty's funeral came round, I looked thin, drawn, and exhausted. This was largely as a result of the stress that both my mind and body were being subjected to. It felt like it was slowly poisoning me.

A smart black jumpsuit with a lace bodice that Matty had sent me just weeks before, as a birthday gift, now became my loose-hanging costume for the funeral. A dark irony and something to hide behind. Many times I've tried to describe how grief felt in those days and the words always seem to fall short. As I woke in the morning, it was the first thought my brain could think, and as I tried to fall asleep at night, I felt scared of everything. His death literally consumed me. My heart felt heavy. A dead weight inside of my chest cavity, dragging me down with each beat. When I cried it ached. That ache was the kind of pain that felt at once tender but also sore.

And yet crying provided relief. So, I cried. I cried at night when the kids were in bed, sleeping soundly despite their own pain. I cried during the day, when I would shut the curtains and cut myself off from the world. I cried when friends or people in the street would ask me how I was. Grief was not simply mental anguish. It was physical for me. And trauma is, too.

When we're exposed to the stress created by traumatic experiences, we have an often visceral bodily reaction.

Trauma is held in both our bodies and our minds, and to heal from it we must find therapeutic modalities that allow us to target both the mental and the physical aspects of our pain.

My familial predispositions are toward anxiety and low mood. These predispositions are likely stored in my DNA. I was aware that this loss was a chronic stressor and one that might lead me to somewhere I was simply unwilling to go. So, I began to look for ways to help myself. I knew I needed to move my body even when I didn't feel like it, and I knew I needed to find purpose and meaning. As well as the predisposition to mental difficulties,

I had become aware of a persistent ache located at my right shoulder blade. Was this my trauma speaking through bodily-felt pain? It nagged on and on for months. Nothing seemed to relieve it. Then, just as suddenly as I had noticed it, I realized I couldn't feel it anymore.

Grief is like that, I think. It lifts incrementally and sometimes imperceptibly with time. One day, as I was standing by the cooker making dinner, to my own surprise I started humming and then singing as I worked. It was a warm day and my mum appeared at my back door. Seeing me standing there, she said, 'Feeling better?' It felt like a crazy question for her to ask. How could I possibly be feeling better? But in that moment, I realized that I actually was.

> No matter how terrible we feel
> or what we go through, emotions
> are temporary and fleeting.

Emotions wax and wane, and with time become less acute. These days I can tell a wave of grief is upon me when I feel that familiar ache on my right shoulder blade. I welcome it with the knowledge that, though grief will travel alongside me in this life, I will in fact be OK.

Trauma and Epigenetics

Knowing what we now know about trauma, epigenetics, too, plays a part. Imagine for a moment being placed under a toxic level of stress for a sustained period. As the body and the brain attempt to cope, certain genes are switched on or off, leading to the body's gene expression being altered over time. This literally exerts changes in our bodies, including the neural pathways in our brains. If this is not addressed, the body can develop disease or difficulties within the brain itself, which can be expressed as depression, anxiety, or some other symptom or problem.

In this way, when we then go on to have children of our own, our altered genes are passed to them – and so the cycle continues. Just as physical health problems often have a genetic component, the genetic code to our own particular 'flavor' of psychological dysfunction or trauma can be passed down the genetic line of succession. And with it, we pass on our symptoms, reactions, and patterns to our offspring.

Reactions to Trauma

To understand our reactions to trauma fully, we must first understand a bit about emotional regulation in the body and the system that governs it. Our nervous system exists firstly to react to stress and then to allow it to dissipate from the body, once we have dealt with the situation from which it arose.

The central nervous system (CNS) consists of the brain, spinal cord, and the nerves, and is designed to regulate how we think, feel, and behave. The CNS can be subdivided into various branches, which include the parasympathetic nervous system (PNS) and the sympathetic nervous system (SNS). Broadly speaking, the PNS governs automatic functions including things like breathing, digestion, arousal, and movement – essentially, anything our body needs to do to survive, but that is out of our conscious control or involuntary. The sympathetic nervous system (SNS) is what governs our 'fight-flight' response.

Now, the 'fight-flight' response is essentially an inbuilt survival mechanism that kicks into action when we perceive ourselves to be under threat. Typically, the types of events that lead to internalized trauma can be threatening. They cause us to respond in ways that ensure our safety and survival.

If I consider my own experience of loss, I remember feeling incredibly fearful in the days that followed. I was in a constant state of hyperarousal, which physiologically was the brain's way of keeping me safe. C.S. Lewis, the author of *The Chronicles of Narnia*, writes in his book *A Grief Observed*, 'No one ever told me that grief felt so like fear. I am not afraid but the sensation is like being afraid.' The trouble was that there was no actual immediate threat to me. But that didn't matter – my nervous system was activated and operating as if there was. This state of hyperarousal isn't good for us over the long term and the stress it induces can be toxic.

It's the same with childhood trauma. If your sympathetic nervous system perceives threat in your environment as a child, then it's on high alert. I've often worked with adults whose threat-activation system has never really turned itself back off. The men in the prison were a good example of that – constantly scanning their environment for the next threat to respond to and always in a state of hyperarousal. For that reason, they often attracted diagnoses of post-traumatic stress disorder (PTSD) in which, as described by *The Diagnostic and Statistical Manual of Mental Disorders* (DSM-5), they react to internal and external cues that bear a similarity to past traumatic events. This is how trauma can keep us in a holding pattern. The 'old' response becomes habitual and isn't necessarily driven by any real threat. To heal, we need to recognize if these types of responses are present for us, so let's look at them in a little more detail.

'Fight' and 'flight' are of course two of the main trauma responses I've observed clinically over the years. They describe the behavioral responses of either standing up to fight your corner or running away. Now, these reactions might not actually mean a stand-up fistfight or a dramatic escape as such; they may be more subtle than that. For example, for some people, their way of 'fighting' when a past trauma is activated is to engage in a pattern of conflict in relationships; while 'fleeing' might look like an avoidance of emotions, or even avoiding the conflict itself by walking away from relationships when things get too hard.

Other trauma responses have become popularized in recent years as adjuncts to the 'fight-flight' concept. These include the 'freeze' response, in which we find ourselves paralyzed. This might look like struggling to make decisions about the future or even making simple day-to-day choices. The final response I want to draw attention to is fawning. I've spoken about this earlier in this book, and it's essentially when we behave in ways to avoid disapproval and criticism from others. Many of my patients acknowledge this as a strategy they've developed in response to overly critical parents.

Schema Patterns

Now, to take this idea of trauma responses and patterns a bit further, I want to introduce you to schemas. I've already mentioned how, when I was developing my skills as a therapist, I knew early on that I wanted to go deeper than traditional CBT allowed me to. Relational therapies made complete sense to me, and understanding people's stories from a relational perspective was something I was good at. Whether through cognitive analytic therapy or schema-based work, I always wanted people to understand what lay beneath.

Psychodynamic therapies like these seek to understand our unconscious processes and unresolved conflicts from the past. These therapies always felt like they helped me to understand my story, too. Schemas are essentially patterns that we develop through our childhood experiences and that reflect the modeling we've received. The goal of schema therapy is therefore to identify within which unhelpful schemas we're operating from and to step out of these where possible. The overarching aim is to reduce the sense of disconnection that schema patterns create with others.

Eighteen early maladaptive schemas were originally presented within schema therapy. More recently, additional schemas have been added that further our clinical understanding of how childhood trauma can manifest in our lives. An example of an early schema is the 'abandonment schema,' in which we've developed a fear of being rejected or abandoned by the people in our life and therefore behave in ways to avoid that possibility. The challenge is that many of the ways in which an abandonment schema might compel us to behave are the exact same sorts of behaviors that could mean people actually do end up rejecting us or leaving us – leading to a self-fulfilling pattern. Another schema that I and many of those I work with struggle with is 'failure schema,' in which we believe we will fail at our endeavors and are inadequate in comparison to others. The behavioral expression of this schema is to procrastinate and avoid your performance being reviewed, therefore reducing the possibility of failure as a whole.

Finding and Growing Your 'Healthy Adult' Mode

When we're doing self-development work, the goal may seem evident. But if I were to ask you now, what would you tell me your aims were? Often, there can be so many that we don't know where to start. Or, conversely, we're simply unsure.

Now, I don't view this type of psychological work as being about trying to shift who you are fundamentally. Rather, I see this work as being about change and growth, while accepting the parts of ourselves that we may have tried to hide in the past. I also want you to feel seen and heard – reassured that whatever you have been through matters. What I don't want you to do is compare your experiences to others, or minimize your pain. I want you to feel validated and empowered just as you are.

Sometimes in this work, the task can feel so great, and the shifts needed to get to where we want to be so monumental, that we struggle to get started. We might read the words and recognize ourselves within them, but feel paralyzed by procrastination, or feel unable to champion change within the context of our busy lives. If this applies to you, one concept that might help you is that of your 'healthy adult.' Coming from schema therapy, the origins of which were detailed in the book *Reinventing Your Life* by psychologists Jeffrey Young and Janet Klosko (1994), the 'healthy adult' is the version of ourselves that we can try to enhance and cultivate. It's considered to be a mode in which we're operating from within our higher self. (Incidentally, 'higher self' is not the pseudo pop-psychology concept I often see it portrayed as on social media.) When I think of developing my higher self, it's about the trend over time of meeting my needs from within the Maslow hierarchy that I mentioned previously. Remember, at the top of that pyramid sits self-actualization – and the 'healthy adult' relates to the self that exists at that highest point.

Your healthy adult knows what your needs are and asks for them to be met unapologetically. So your aim now is to strengthen and grow your healthy adult skills and abilities. This is not an overnight change, but one of slow, steady, consistent progress. For example, almost a year after my mum returned from her studies as a young woman, she began to uncover her own healthy adult, and kept going until she found a way back to herself. I myself have had to keep on connecting with my healthy adult to override the unrelenting standards that occasionally hold me back.

One of the questions that I frequently put to my clients may be useful to you when it comes to connecting with your own 'healthy adult.' When faced with life's challenges, just ask yourself, 'Am I operating from within my healthy adult mode?' If the answer is no, this then begs the question: which mode are you operating from?

Schema therapy has further applications here as, when we build our awareness, we can usually start to notice and label our other modes. For example, schema therapy would typically suggest that everyone can express core child modes, too, which are associated with particular schemas or patterns of relating. These modes include 'vulnerable child,' 'angry child,' 'impulsive/undisciplined child,' and 'happy child.' The idea is that the healthy adult within us can gently parent and nurture our vulnerable child, discipline and set fair limits for our angry or impulsive child, and moderate the other unhelpful ways of coping that we use to hide the unmet needs of our childhood.

The Healthy Adult and Family Patterns

I'm incredibly proud that while I was writing this book, my mum and I were able to have a conversation about our past. When talking about how she had parented me in the context of the childhood messaging that she herself had received, she acknowledged that she often focused on the wrong things. These days, this occasionally manifests in different ways.

That very morning, in fact, she reflected that she'd told my daughter she 'must stick in at school' – 'stick in' meaning to do well.

My daughter responded, 'But what if I don't want to do well at school?'

My mum replied, 'But you have to' – as if this was a statement of absolute truth. She was aware that this was perhaps unhelpful, but felt compelled to say it anyway, because it was what she knew and had been told herself.

I'm aware that I do this myself and, like me, you might experience this in those moments when you hear your own voice and realize you've internalized someone else's and think, like I often do, 'I sound just like my mum!' And of course that's how modeling works: We begin to think and behave as our model did.

She and I talked about how we can hold on so tightly to our kids' 'success' that we act in ways that are counterproductive to them achieving it. We get attached to what we believe they 'should' be doing and forget to ask whether it in fact makes them happy. My mum knew what this was like. She had walked that path, too. Today, I try to parent my daughter not by aligning myself with the 'shoulds' of this life, or of my own conditioning, but by what her needs are. I truly hope she and I might have a similar conversation one day, in which she tells me that for the most part this approach served her well.

TRAUMA TOOLKIT

Before progressing to Part III, I'd like you to put together your own personalized 'trauma toolkit.' When complete, it will consist of all the tools and strategies you'll need to ensure that you're grounded and feeling mentally strong for the work ahead.

To make a start, take out your journal and answer the questions below:

- *If you've done any self-development or psychological work before, what practices helped previously to support you in the work?*

- *What other practices might you seek to add to your toolkit now?*

- *Should your emotions feel overwhelming in any psychological work, it's important you know how to regulate them and stay grounded. Consider two to three grounding practices and write them down. These might include using guided meditation practices, or harnessing the power of getting into nature to interrupt trauma patterns and regulate your emotions, or perhaps just something as simple as sharing your struggles with a trusted friend.*

- *Consider setting yourself up with an accountability partner – someone you trust who you can share your intentions with around this work and check in with. They'll be able to help you remain focused while also offer a listening ear should the work become challenging.*

- *You might wish to join my online Facebook community and share your progress with the group. You will be able to request free access by searching for 'Know Your Own Psychology' and making a join request.*

PART III

The Tools
to Heal

CHAPTER 7

Telling Your Own Story

Even as a little girl, I loved stories. I enjoyed guessing ahead and wondering where the narrative was headed next. I was also curious and wanted to make sense of the decisions characters made and why they behaved as they did. I loved books, and my dad made me a makeshift wooden storage drawer that fitted underneath my bed. All my books lived there and every night we'd pull out the drawer, select a story, and read for a while before bed. I treasured those times with my dad.

One of my favorite books offered several options at the end of each chapter. You got to decide what happened by picking alternative versions of the story. It was such a simple concept, yet it brought me hours of entertainment as we'd read and re-read with different variations of the story each time we did. Strangely, I no longer remember the details of what the story was about, but I do remember the colorful hot air balloon soaring over the tiny characters on the book cover. This may be the beginnings of where my love for psychological formulation began – an example of how the 'sliding door' moments of our lives can alter our trajectories forever.

Formulation, in psychological terms, simply means telling the story of how and why someone is struggling with a particular psychological difficulty at a particular time, in an attempt to allow them to change the trajectory of that story. In my training appraisals at the end of each clinical placement, formulation was always a core strength of mine. I found that the process of meeting someone new, curiously gathering information about their life, reflecting, and then assimilating that information into some semblance of order came easily to me – formulating a story that shed light on their struggles and would ultimately help them to move forward positively.

As a clinical psychologist, I was trained to work my way through this process across a client's developmental lifespan from childhood to adulthood, and into their twilight years. I was often struck by how often, after conducting an assessment and formulation, and then sharing my understanding of the 'story' with a client, they would reflect that they'd never looked at their life in that way before. The 'penny drop' moments were so obviously meaningful to people that I realized even just shifting their perspective by sharing a formulation could be a powerful precursor to making change happen in their lives.

However, telling our own story can be hard to do, especially if we don't have a compassionate and supportive guide at our disposal. Firstly, it is ours, so it can be challenging to zoom out and see the wider context. Secondly, it is emotional and that can cause us to avoid examining it, as we seek to remain in comfortable ignorance. Most of us know intuitively that any type of self-development work has the potential to hold up a mirror to our issues and flaws, and show us a different route forward.

When we know a thing, we cannot simply
travel back to the time before we knew it.

It's like the quote often attributed to Maya Angelou that says, 'Do the best you can until you know better. Then when you know better, do better.'

Psychological work asks us to increase our knowledge and, armed with that knowledge, to do better by ourselves and others, too. If we know a thing and cannot engage with it fully, or make the behavioral changes that our new knowledge requires of us, this creates what psychologists call 'cognitive dissonance.' Cognitive dissonance is essentially the discomfort created when we continue to behave in ways that are not aligned with our belief system or values.

The reason for telling you this is simple: If you don't feel ready to shift your perspective and look at things differently, then you may want to pause here and return at a future date. I don't want to create cognitive dissonance for you before you are ready to face the work required. And even working on 'small t' trauma requires readiness and stability.

Phased Trauma Work

Though self-development work is not the same as the sort of trauma work you would complete alongside a psychologist or other mental health professional, I'd like you to think about the work I'm asking you to do in a similar way. In trauma work, it's entirely normal to work in a phase-based way. Phase one is about establishing safety and stabilization. It's crucial to give yourself a robust foundation that includes a support network to lean on and an established trauma toolkit of strategies and healthy coping mechanisms. The aim is that you feel mentally strong before you begin.

For some people, establishing this foundation can take many months and even years. If you recognize that you are currently in a fight, flight or freeze state, or that day-to-day stressors are causing you to struggle to cope, then the timing for this work needs to be carefully considered and perhaps even postponed. This is because the second phase of psychological work, in which you delve into the memories of your traumatic experiences, can create not just dissonance, but may dysregulate your emotional state in unhelpful ways. This is not something that any psychologist would recommend without a client first having the skills and strategies in place to manage any difficulties, should they arise.

The final phase of this work is integration, in which you learn to incorporate shifts in your thinking and behavior into your life as a whole.

> This healing may be accompanied by
> new hopes and dreams for the future.

Only you will be able to assess where you are and whether you feel ready to begin the work. It's important to understand that working through the contents of this book is not the same as collaborating with a trained mental health professional, so please seek support from one, should you require it. If you haven't yet completed the trauma toolkit exercise in the previous chapter, I would encourage you to do so.

Now, with all that said, in this chapter I am going to outline the component parts of good psychological work. You will be invited to think like a psychologist – to tell your story and formulate how it has contributed to your challenges in the here and now. The assessment and formulation exercise brings together the sort of cognitive behavioral and relational components spoken about in earlier chapters, and I will offer additional points of reflection.

The Components of Good Psychological Work

The four components required for good psychological work are:

1. Assessment

2. Formulation

3. Treatment

4. Evaluation

Psychological assessment essentially means pulling together all the information and experiences of our lives, to understand and make sense of them. It's the first step of any psychological work. This may seem straightforward enough, but, in my experience, it can be difficult to collate the multitude of experiences from across our lives in a simple and linear way that makes sense. It's not unusual for the assessments that I conduct in my clinical practice to take several sessions. Often, people move around their stories in a haphazard way, leaping from the present to past events, and jumping in and out of different periods like a time-traveler without the correct coordinates. Our memories may come to us in fits and starts, or in a piecemeal fashion. This might reflect a prior self-protection mechanism, which saw us locking away our painful memories.

In telling our stories, it can seem like we're struggling to create order from the chaos. I think this is perhaps reflective of how our minds assimilate our experiences, making it hard for us to understand the true meaning and impact of our unique sequence of life events. Consequently, you might need time to immerse yourself in this phase of the work, as it will likely allow memories to come forward and reflections or thoughts to emerge. Depending on the complexity of your 'story' and the events in your life, it may take many hours, or even days, for you to complete this part of the work.

One of the tools that might be useful for you here is a timeline. A timeline is simply a visual representation of your life from birth until the present day. I find that most people agree it's helpful to have this laid out visually for them, and to see their life as a whole, as opposed to isolated incidents or events. In this way, they begin to understand the integrated nature of their psychology and how it develops through time and experience. Your timeline will include the key moments of your life, such as your birth, schooling, any significant losses, or key events. I've included a rough example to give you an idea of how it might look.

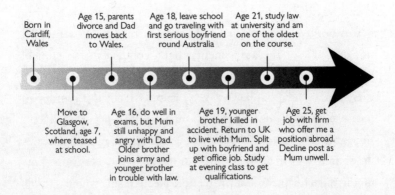

A sample timeline

Adverse Childhood Experiences

To help you complete your own timeline, I want to introduce you to a study that has highlighted key areas for consideration. In psychological assessment work, we are often looking for adverse childhood experiences or 'ACEs' in people's developmental backgrounds to understand their impact. Adverse childhood experiences tend to be the 'big T' events of our lives.

The original ACEs study looked at the relationship between various categories of traumatic experience and risk behavior, health status and disease (Felitti et al., 1998). What they found was that higher numbers of adverse childhood experiences showed a graded relationship to adult disease. In other words, the more trauma you have been exposed to, the greater the likelihood of you experiencing challenges to your overall health and well-being in adult life. A further example of the strength of the mind-body connection. I have listed the 10 questions that outline adverse childhood experiences below:

1. Did you feel that you didn't have enough to eat, had to wear dirty clothes, or had no one to protect or take care of you?

2. Did you lose a parent through divorce, abandonment, death, or other reason?

3. Did you live with anyone who was depressed, mentally ill, or attempted suicide?

4. Did you live with anyone who had a problem with drinking or using drugs, including prescription drugs?

5. Did your parents or the adults in your home ever hit, punch, beat, or threaten to harm each other?

6. Did you live with anyone who went to jail or prison?

7. Did a parent or adult in your home ever swear at you, insult you, or put you down?

8. Did a parent or adult in your home ever hit, beat, kick, or physically hurt you in any way?

9. Did you feel that no one in your family loved you or thought you were special?

10. Did you experience any unwanted sexual contact (such as fondling, or oral/anal/vaginal intercourse or penetration)?

Though not all the experiences highlighted by the ACEs study will resonate with those of you who choose to read this book, knowing more about them will help guide you in developing your timeline.

I also want to highlight two of the ACEs laid out above. Though they appear less shocking than most of the categories, for me they get to the heart of the 'unseen' trauma that, all too often, we have ignored or didn't understand was trauma in the first place. The first of these is item 7: 'Did an adult ever swear at you, insult you, or put you down?' The second is item 9: 'Did you feel that no one in your family loved you or thought you were special?' The reason for highlighting these items over the others is that they seem more open to uncertainty. Intuitively, the other items are more binary: Did this awful neglect, abuse, or parental death happen in your life or did it not? These two items, by contrast, are more difficult to quantify. More nuanced.

The reason for this, in my view, is clear. It's because these items, over the others, are truly relational. They speak to the disrupted attachment and the intricacies of our relationships. The ways in which an adult may have insulted us, or put us down, may actually have been quite subtle; so subtle, in fact, that perhaps we didn't truly see it as children. And perhaps it was not so obvious that other adults would have noticed it either. Of course, other, far worse abuses go unnoticed, too, but when those abuses are uncovered they are far less open to being dismissed. Additionally, not feeling loved or special is the meaning that we ourselves make of our experiences. That's simply not something that someone else can determine for you.

Please use your growing awareness of your own story to fill out your timeline. When your timeline is complete, you will have laid out your life before you in a diagram of sorts. In our busy lives, it's often challenging to take the time to reflect and to see our lives from this angle, so once you have your timeline in front of you, I'd like you to spend a while reflecting on it, and to refer to it when you move on to the next step of formulating and telling your story.

Variations on Formulation

In psychology, there are many differing therapeutic modalities and treatment approaches. As I've explained, I find that relational attachment-based work is particularly effective and meaningful for those I work with. In this same way, there can be different approaches to formulation that align with the type of therapy selected. I tend to use a combination of cognitive behavioral approaches to formulation, adding relational components for depth and greater understanding.

In cognitive behavioral therapy, we often use a model known as the 5Ps. The 5Ps is a framework you can use to formulate and tell your story under the headings of the following key aspects. These are:

1. Presenting factors

2. Predisposing factors

3. Precipitating factors

4. Perpetuating factors

5. Protective factors

I'll go through each of these factors in turn, so that you'll have a better understanding of them that will help you to complete your self-assessment and formulation.

Presenting Factors

These are the factors or difficulties that you might show up with in therapy, wanting to change. They are the here-and-now reasons why you've picked up this book. Perhaps you have at one time felt broken and the book's title spoke to you? Perhaps you're struggling with the symptoms of poor mental health, such as anxiety or low mood? Psychologists think about this as the presenting problem: Essentially, why is this person here today in my consulting room? So, ask yourself: Why I am reading this book today, and what is it about how I think and feel that I would like to change?

Predisposing Factors

These are the factors that make you more susceptible to psychological difficulties. They are the biological, environmental, and/or personality factors we would consider that may make it more likely for you to struggle with some psychological difficulty. This might refer to the genetic component of particular psychological disorders, or trauma, as outlined previously. Generally, they can be thought of as the factors that may have contributed to the person's problem.

Precipitating Factors

These are the factors that triggered your current difficulties. What has been happening in the preceding months or weeks? Perhaps you've been under a significant degree of stress? Perhaps you've lost your job, or are unsure of your direction in life? Maybe, as in my own case, you've suffered a significant loss that has made you re-evaluate the way you are living, or that has caused a crisis that must be attended to. These are the factors that may have initiated or exacerbated the current problem.

Perpetuating Factors

These are the factors that maintain your current difficulties, keeping you stuck. Often, the factors that had an impact at the beginning of our psychological problems are not the same ones that perpetuate them now. These factors could include issues like a lack of family support, or being unable to access therapy in a timely way. They may also be things such as lack of motivation, or struggling to define your identity without the difficulties you're currently living with. If these factors aren't addressed, they usually lead to the problem getting worse.

Protective Factors

These factors are the things in your life that are helpful and guard against further decline in your psychological functioning. They may include things such as a healthy social network. They can also include factors such as employment, taking any medication that you require in a timely way, having good problem-solving skills, or previous experience of managing psychological difficulty.

Sometimes, we can make a further addition to this type of CBT formulation and the model becomes a 6P formulation. The sixth factor is that of predictive factors. This is a useful addition to the 5P model, as it asks us to consider what's likely to happen if we don't address the presenting issues.

So, let me ask you this: If the challenges you face and the difficult emotions and symptoms you're experiencing are not addressed, where will you be in six months' time, or a year, or five years? If the reason you picked up this book and the issues you wish to change are left unresolved, what will your life look like in the future? This factor is essentially asking us to consider whether we are willing to leave things as they are, based on a prediction of what life might look like if we do. If, after reading this book, you do nothing, change nothing, are you happy with the future prediction of what your life might look like? If the answer is no, then let's keep going to figure out what you need to change and how you're going to get there.

Now that you have an understanding of a CBT approach to formulation using the framework I've outlined, I want you to work through these factors in turn and identify what these are for you. Your previously completed timeline will help you consider what was going on for you at certain time points in your life. You can simply write these out in your journal or the workbook available to download from my website.

Relational Formulation

You may recall how in Chapter 5 I outlined my belief that if we recognize a relational problem in our past, we need a relational solution to tackle it effectively. This is why I've always been drawn toward relational attachment-based therapies. So many of my clients presented with difficulties beyond the scope of what CBT seemed able to address, as they needed to dig deeper to the relational patterns that in turn shaped up their thinking about themselves, others, and the world.

Part of that relational solution entails developing a relational formulation. Earlier in this book, I outlined a number of core concepts related to relational formulation, and how we need to utilize psychological concepts of reciprocity and social modeling theory to make sense of our familial relationships. With these principles in mind, the first thing you are going to do now is to identify someone who was an influential early caregiver for you to formulate. You and they make up the relational dyad, or pairing (*see Chapter 4*). Remember how, in Cognitive Analytic Therapy (CAT), the reciprocal role procedure (RRP) is a model that depicts this relationship with the parent/caregiver, with the adult in the top pole or position and the child in the bottom pole or position (*see Chapter 5*)? I'd like you to put yourself in the position of the child, and you'll then need to consider how you might describe your parent or caregiver. Were they kind and controlling, or loving and angry, for example?

The key here is not what they would
say about how they parented you,
but how you experienced it.

Remember, perception is key.

Of course, it's important to understand that other people may experience you differently to how you think you are, too, yet the more self-aware you are, the more accurate your view of yourself will nevertheless be. I'd recommend focusing on your childhood first and using that to extrapolate forward in time, working from your past to your future. The model will begin to make more sense over time as you apply it.

You can formulate your relationships in the same way in relation to all your different caregivers, and apply this approach to situations in your adult life now; it's a simple and practical way to map relationships. Then, consider how to 'exit' any unhelpful relational patterns, as I'll explain shortly.

In order to demonstrate how you might self-formulate using this relational mapping process, I'm going to use myself as an example and consider this in relation to my own children and myself, and how they relate to me, given my parenting style. This feels like a vulnerable share, but one I'm willing to offer as I take you through the relational aspects of formulating and show you how powerful this can be as an aid to both your understanding and what might be showing up in your life in the here and now.

When it comes to my own example, I'm naturally going to be looking at this from my own perspective, based on the here and now of my life. Now, given what you already know about my history, you'll be aware that I can be perfectionistic and hold high expectations of both myself and others. I believe this is often experienced by others around me as control. Despite this, I'm also loving and kind. I am rule-bound and tend to feel anxious in situations where it could seem that rules aren't being followed.

If I asked my daughter and perhaps even my twin boys about how this behavior affects them, I'm almost certain they would tell me that I can be 'too strict.' For me personally, being strict is undoubtedly about safety, control, and predictability. While this is something I'm still working on, I also know that boundaries are important and that kids often want more autonomy than they're actually able to cope with at a given developmental stage. My awareness of these 'issues' in the way that I am and can be around others involves a precarious balancing act. And for those parents out there, parenting is by far the hardest job I've ever had. Self-awareness will help you in this.

So let me paint the picture of how I would formulate this in a relational way. I will use two of the words I've used to describe my parenting and how I can 'be.'

Remember, words and language matter.

However, sometimes it can be hard to pinpoint the exact word, or one can feel too much; whenever we use adjectives to describe ourselves and others, an overwhelming feeling can rise up of our not wanting to 'blame' whoever we are formulating alongside ourselves. And it's entirely normal to feel this way. Try not to overthink this and remember this isn't a blame game. (At the end of the chapter, I'll offer possible example words for you to try out in your own formulation.)

To return to my example, as you can see from the diagram, I've used the words 'controlling' and 'loving.' I suspect the reality of this for my children and for other people potentially around me is that they feel my warmth and love. But they also feel the control that I try, at times, to exert over situations.

Adult (Me)

**CONTROLLING
&
LOVING**

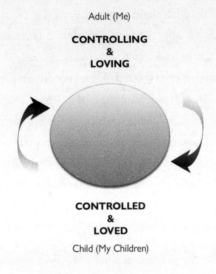

**CONTROLLED
&
LOVED**

Child (My Children)

*A formulation of my relationship
with my children*

Through my modeling, they develop a felt sense of what it is to feel loved and controlled. And as they develop that felt sense, they are also observing my behaviors of love and control. Both these feelings and behaviors will be internalized by my children and become part of their own relational repertoire as adults. Psychologists call this an internal working model, which is essentially a mental representation or blueprint of our self, others, and relationships that govern how we respond, including our thoughts, feeling and behaviors in situations in which attachment is relevant (Bretherton and Munholland, 1999). We also know that these models impact our social cognition, emotional regulation, relationship dynamics, and psychological well-being (Mikulincer and Shaver, 2016).

Feeling loved is, of course, a positive experience. If this pattern is internalized, it will allow my children not only to feel loved by me and others, but to direct that love back at themselves, and to go out into the world and love others. The internal working model will have done its delicate job of giving my children a map to work from. More than that, it will be spread to other areas of their lives, too.

Feeling controlled, on the other hand, is usually an unwelcome experience. Yet if this pattern is internalized, it does the same thing. It teaches my children what it is to feel controlled and to direct that control back at themselves, and to go out into the world and control others. The internal working model has again done its job, but the effects are not necessarily as positive. If my children experience control as emotionally intolerable in some way they may fluctuate between these two relational poles of either being controlled or being controlling. If the feeling of being controlled becomes too great and the emotions that arise feel overwhelming, they might 'flip' 180 degrees and attempt to step into the top relational pole. This is their attempt to take back some of the control and avoid the distress experienced in the bottom position.

As I try to navigate parenting a pre-teen daughter, this situation is a reality that I'm living each day currently. There are, of course, degrees to the extent to which 'control' becomes a problem. As a comparison, there is likely to be a stark difference between the challenges that control will exert on my children's lives and the difficulties around control experienced by many of the men I worked with in the Scottish Prison Service. It's individual and it's complex. It's multifactorial and nuanced.

The good news is that once we have mapped a relationship, we can then consider exit strategies to help us break unhelpful patterns. For example, rather than continuously cycling round and round in a 'control or be controlled' spiral, the goal would be to work out the best way to step out of the unhealthy reciprocal role procedure, internal working model, or pattern.

The same goes for me as a parent now. I need to work out where I'm being too controlling with my children, and consider how I might choose to step out and relax the rules a little. And that's while still holding age-appropriate boundaries. What did I tell you? It's the hardest job I've ever had. People often ask me if it's helpful having psychological knowledge like this to apply to my own life. While I'll always agree it is, I do have to check myself for a tendency to overanalyze circumstances. I know that mostly I am better off for knowing. But with knowledge and understanding can come a degree of suffering, particularly if we are behaving in ways that are incongruent with our own values.

Personality and Relational Models

Now, before we move on to do your own relational model mapping and psychological formulation, I want to highlight the links between personality and relational models. Our personalities form across our childhood development, and because of what we experience, some of us have a larger number of relational models or 'ways of being' that we can draw on, while some of us will have a more limited number of relational models. For some of us, particular models will be more dominant than others, as depicted in the diagram below.

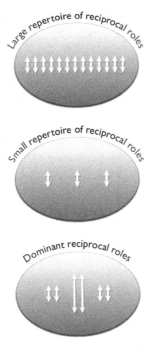

Large repertoire of reciprocal roles

Small repertoire of reciprocal roles

Dominant reciprocal roles

Ways in which some of our relational models
can be more dominant than others

Another way to think about this is that if we have been modeled very limited 'ways of being,' then that's all we can draw on to utilize as we try to relate to ourselves and others. This can mean that our 'ways of being' can become quite fixed and hard to change and shift. The overall goal is to become more adaptive and flexible by adding to our relational repertoire, and/or by reducing our reliance on certain relational models.

Getting to Grips with Relational Formulation

The diagram overleaf shows you how the building blocks of how relationship models form. In the top position, or pole, sits the parent or caregiver. In the bottom position, or pole, sits the child (in this instance, you when you were younger).

Over time, we internalize the patterns
we learn and then we take them with
us into our adult relationships.

Our goal is to work out if these relational patterns are unhelpful.

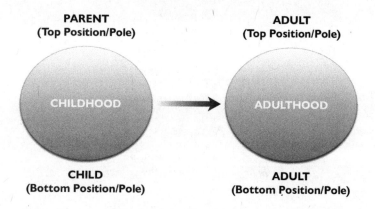

The building blocks of relationship models

The next step lies in the process of defining the language we will use to describe the specifics of how we experienced our relationships in childhood. Remember that most people can usually identify both helpful and unhelpful relational models. The diagram below shows how both helpful and unhelpful patterns are modeled by parents and caregivers, according to social modeling theory.

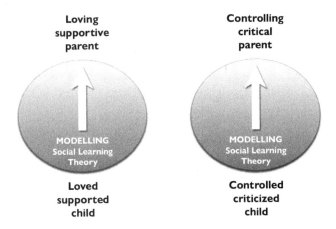

Examples of helpful and unhelpful relational models

The last step in the process allows you to consider how the more unhelpful relational models may have impacted your behavior today as an adult. When we have internalized an unhelpful relational pattern in childhood, like the one shown in the diagram below, and this is activated or triggered by an event in adulthood, we may well respond in unhelpful ways.

In this example, when the person feels criticized or controlled in any way, this forces them into the bottom position, where their emotions can feel overwhelming. Usually, people respond by either exiting the cycle in unhealthy ways that allow them to 'numb out' the emotional response, through the use of alcohol or drugs, for example, or even simple avoidance, or they do what they know and 'flip' into the top position of being controlling and critical in response. This makes them feel better in the short term.

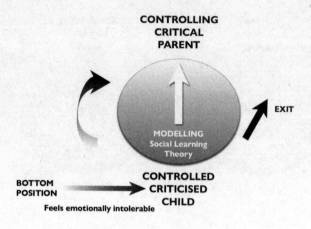

*Exiting the cycle in unhealthy ways or
'flipping to the opposite pole'*

Identifying Your Key Relational Models – and HEAL

I realize that this may feel complicated, so let's try to simplify it a little more. Opposite are some more examples of helpful and unhelpful relational models. These examples are offered to help you think about your own models. When working on these, you can also use any words or language that make sense to you.

OK, now that you hopefully have a clearer understanding of relational models, I'd like you to try some relational mapping for yourself, using the self-formulation exercise at the end of this chapter. Remember, this is simply a way to map out the key relationship models from your childhood and it's about telling your story.

However, before you begin the exercise, I'd like to take a moment to think about how to make this exercise, and the

Helpful parent–child relationship RRPs

Unhelpful parent–child relationship RRPs

Unhelpful adult–adult relationship RRPs

*Different forms that helpful and unhelpful
relational models can take*

others that follow, truly meaningful. To an extent, I think that psychological work can sometimes formalize working on the self in a way that can be unhelpful. The language and psychological terminology can feel very medicalized and off-putting. Words such as 'assessment,' 'formulation,' 'treatment,' and 'evaluation' can sound far removed from the human reality of the pain that you might be suffering. Therefore, I wanted to offer a slightly alternative framework of thinking about what it is that this work requires of you.

Making the work meaningful matters, both in terms of the meaning you make of your past and how you make it all make sense.

> When I consider what I want
> you to get out of this book, it's
> simple. I want you to heal.

And so, I'm going to offer you a simple way of thinking about the steps I'll be asking you to take as you complete the work of the chapters in this third section of the book. It takes the form of a four-step HEAL framework, which aligns roughly with the key components of good psychological work:

- Highlight the significant experiences of your life (*assessment-focused*).

- Engage with your reality fully to make sense of it (*formulation-focused*).

- Attune to your feelings related to these life experiences (*treatment-focused*).

- Let it lift (*future-focused*).

Next Steps

In this chapter, you've been invited to pull together and work on your own psychological assessment and formulation. This incorporates a number of different approaches in an eclectic mix designed to make the most of this opportunity to build your psychological awareness. Review the areas described in the exercise below and make sure you have completed the work for each section in your journal. Alternatively, you can download the accompanying worksheet for this section from the link on page xvi.

So far, we've explored how to tell your own story through using psychological frameworks for assessment and formulation. I hope this has allowed you to pinpoint and begin to make sense of your life story, and how it may have been impacting your overall psychological well-being.

Now you need to know what to do with what you've learned. In Chapter 8, therefore, we'll be considering the emotions and the 'suffering' that arise as a result of psychological work and what to do about that.

WRITING UP YOUR FORMULATION

Before we move on any further, it's now time to pull it all together. You are going to use the following prompts to write and develop your own psychological formulation in your journal or in the free accompanying workbook available at the link on page xvi.

Timeline: Complete a timeline of your life as outlined earlier, on page 138.

6Ps Formulation: Complete a CBT-based formulation using the 6Ps framework:

- **Presenting factors**: *What are your presenting problems? Remember that these might be things like your mood and the challenges you currently face. These are essentially things you want to change.*

- **Predisposing factors**: *What factors do you think might make you more susceptible to psychological difficulties? They can include biological, environmental, and/or personality traits, or the past traumas you have faced.*

- **Precipitating factors**: *What has happened recently to upset you emotionally and make life feel more difficult?*

- **Perpetuating factors**: *What is making it difficult for you to move on from the situation you are in and the emotions you are feeling?*

- **Protective factors**: *What factors are helping to make life feel more manageable or offer you sources of comfort and support?*

- **Predicative factors**: *If things continue as they are, without change, what situation might you find yourself in?*

Relational Mapping: Using the template opposite (or you can replicate in a notebook), fill in your own parent–child relational model(s). Use as many of the models as you need/want, examining each significant caring figure in your life. Try to identify the key relational patterns and who they relate to. Then consider how these relational patterns could be showing up in your life today. Who does this pattern relate to? How would you like this to be different? I recommend you think about, and map, both the helpful and unhelpful patterns. For more help, see the downloadable workbook on my website, using the link on page xvi.

Helpful/Unhelpful Parent–Child Relational Model

Helpful/Unhelpful Parent–Child Relational Model

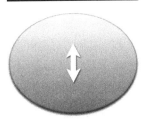

Helpful/Unhelpful Parent–Child Relational Model

CHAPTER 8

Releasing Shame and Cultivating Compassion

When I was roughly midway through my psychology degree, I remember being given several options to choose from for the essay credit of a module. If I recall correctly, the module was on emotions. Two essay questions stood out to me, the first because it seemed unusual and interesting. It involved selecting the main character from the popular novel *Trainspotting* by Irvine Welsh and completing a full character assessment, including key events, the character's motivations, and the emotions that drove their behavior. Looking back, it was really a psychological formulation of sorts, I just didn't realize it then.

The other essay option that stood out was about shame. The reason it appeared so noticeable, I think, was because of how short and simplistic the essay question seemed. But then I thought about it. I seemed to know instinctively that this was a topic that might look simple on the surface but would likely open a cavern of underlying ideas and complicated sub-topics.

In the end, I opted for the *Trainspotting* essay and received a decent mark for a character assessment of the main protagonist, Mark Renton. Despite my good mark, on reflection I think my choice was telling. Even though I wasn't being asked to outline my own experiences for the purposes of the essay in the second option, I was obviously avoiding the universally experienced emotion of shame. Why? Well, I believe that shame has a unique power over us as human beings. It compels us to avoid, shrink, and hide. As we feel it rise from the pit of our stomach, we want to quell the power it has over us and push it back down.

Think of the last time you felt shameful about something. It's an incredibly uncomfortable emotion to sit with and hold. In my view, shame is by far the most destructive emotion, and I've seen it keep people in cycles of unhelpful and self-punishing behavior for years. Clinically, I've known many clients come to session and share personal experiences with me that they describe feeling 'guilty' about. When explored, I've often found that it is shame that lies beneath. Where guilt is typically a feeling of having done something 'bad' or that we believe we shouldn't have done, shame is a feeling of 'I am a bad person.'

You may notice the similarity of this statement to the core beliefs I outlined in Chapter 5. This is why shame keeps us stuck. Its very existence colors how we view ourselves and how we fear others may view us, too. We learn to hide away the 'parts' of ourselves that we're ashamed of so that we'll remain acceptable to others. In this way, slowly but surely, shame silences us, as we travel further and further from the truest version of who we are. The longer that continues, the worse our disconnection to others can become, and, with it, our feelings of loneliness and differentiation from others.

Shame separates us from the pack by making us feel 'different.' Some of us may be aware of this disconnect and the loneliness that shame may have created in our lives. Others may be quite heavily defended to that reality, or not even aware that it's shame that is partially to blame for perpetuating our problems.

> Whatever your current level of awareness of shame, I can tell you this confidently: To be free of your past, you must find a way to release shame, wherever you find it.

Shame is something that we've all likely experienced at various points in our lives. My first recollection of shame as a child came after I did something quite risky and out of character for me. Rather impulsively, I took it upon myself to climb all the way out of our semi-detached house's bathroom window onto our single-story kitchen extension. The extension would have been eight-feet high, and I was around nine or 10 years old. From this vantage point, I was able to take in a whole new view of our small garden, with its rows of tatties (potatoes), which my dad planted each year, and the stream that ran past our back fence.

I don't remember much about the incident itself. Retrospectively, it seems that being caught by my parents had limited emotional impact on me; otherwise I might have remembered more of the event itself. What I do remember is how awful I felt when I was scolded for it later that night by the leader of my junior Girl Guides group. My parents must have told her, and she felt it important to impress on me how dangerous what I'd done could have been. In front of the other members of my pack, I felt so small and, well, bad. Like I'd done something utterly terrible. As

I stood there listening to her tell me off, I could feel the many sets of eyes staring at me from all over the church hall where we met each Monday night. I was a 'sixer,' my first leadership position, and I had done something that made me lesser somehow.

It's a simple childhood example and pales in comparison to the stories of some of my clients, who have internalized shame after experiences of sexual abuse, neglect, or other trauma. But it was my introduction to shame and the beginning of the dumbing down of what appeared to be a risky impulsive streak somewhere inside me. I had broken the rules. That was bad and I felt it.

Over the years that followed, I was shamed by boys in school for my underdeveloped prepubescent body. I was shamed for my enthusiasm for learning. I was shamed for my need to play by the rules, and I was shamed for believing in myself. I was bullied and pushed out of friendship groups, as many of you may also have experienced, in the predictable relational exchanges of school life and amid growing maturity.

My high school years were particularly formative for me. At one point, I remember feeling so unacceptable to my peers that my main goal in life was to get through each day without attracting attention from any direction. Like a chameleon, I blended in to match the wallpaper of whatever space I found myself in. Sometimes it worked. Mostly it didn't. My sense of shame compelled me to hide myself away and hope for the best outcome – which was to go completely unnoticed and forgotten. I wanted desperately to be invisible.

The shadows of these experiences still follow me today. Though I have built my psychology practice largely through social media, visibility remains hard for me. Some days, it feels challenging to invite people into my life. It feels threatening to open myself up to criticism and others' opinions. But, through experience and my training, I feel much more strongly about the importance of sharing my own vulnerabilities, in the hope that you might feel able to take my lead and do the same. I do still struggle with holding appropriate boundaries, primarily with the people I am close to, because I don't want to let them down. I still say 'yes' too often and 'no' too infrequently. And I continue to care too much about what those who seek to criticize me think, though this is getting less all the time.

And then, of course, there was Matty's death. If someone had told me that one day my young husband would die an untimely death, I could not have predicted that feeling shameful would have been such a prominent feature of the experience. You may rightly ask what on earth I would have to feel shameful about. The truth is, nothing. But that is not how our minds work. In situations like this, it's common to ruminate and overthink. In 'stages of grief' language, I spent hours bargaining with myself about the what-ifs of it all. What if we hadn't shared that bottle of wine before bed that night? What if I hadn't gone to bed earlier than he had? What if I had commenced life support before the ambulance crew arrived? What if he hadn't been working away from home, with all the physical stress it placed on his body? I supported his decision to do that. Me. What if I could have done something – anything – to prevent his death? I felt shameful about all of it.

What if, what if, what if...? Eventually, you come to realize that no amount of bargaining with yourself alters the finality of death. He wasn't coming back, no matter how long or hard I berated myself. The same can be said for your trauma. You can't think yourself a different reality from that which you've already lived. And you can't heal without acknowledging shame and learning to loosen its constricting grip.

Like a choke hold, shame will starve you of oxygen until your body cannot breathe and gives in, lying limp on the floor.

Like my mum before me, I was in danger of allowing these thoughts and feelings to take over. To send me into hiding.

In the end, it was my children who allowed me to see the importance of showing myself grace. I was now their whole world. The space once occupied by their dad would now be filled by too few bittersweet memories and a finite number of photographs. I owed it to myself – and to them – to find the compassion to forgive myself for whatever new reason I invented that made me even partially responsible for his death. And though not of his choosing, I owed it to myself to forgive him for leaving us. Leaving me to cope with his loss, and to support our children through it, felt like the most selfish thing he had ever done. There were moments I was utterly furious with him. The irony of it all, of course, was that the only person I wanted to speak to about it and seek solace from was him. He was gone, but I resolved that I wouldn't be consumed by the anger I felt. 'Don't look back in anger' became my internal mantra and allowed me to begin the process of living compassionately through our loss.

With time, I realized that I had nothing to berate myself for, or feel shameful about. But what about when we know we have behaved in ways that we're not proud of?

ACCOUNTING FOR OUR OFFENCES

In the cognitive behavioral programs I facilitated in the prison, the inmates' 'offence accounts' formed a particularly powerful example of how shame can impact people. Those men who had found themselves on one of the rehabilitation programs would often be asked to provide an account of the offence that had brought them to jail. While delivering these programs, I helped many men to write and read their offence accounts within a group environment.

Neither before this, nor in the 18 years since, have I witnessed such extreme expressions of shame. For some men, they experienced their own crimes as reprehensible. I recall one group participant who, after reading his offence account, broke down sobbing and pleaded for help to change. He felt appalled by his past behavior and powerless to change his future without support. He was in the right place and had allowed himself the vulnerability of asking for help, and being honest about both what he had done and his fears for what was to come for him.

Another man offered an entirely contrasting reaction to his offence account. He gave a brief, not entirely accurate account of the offence, and appeared to struggle to take responsibility for his crimes. His account lacked vulnerability and transparency, and he gave little consideration to his future. He was heavily defended from the reality of what he had been convicted of.

The interesting thing is, the second example is in many ways the more natural human reaction. All of us understand that feeling when we are ashamed of something. Often, we struggle to acknowledge our behavior or to be honest about it. We feel compelled to hide behind excuses or inaccuracies.

I recall this particular example because this man's reaction was so extreme. As the session continued, he became angry, directing his rage toward me. I no longer remember exactly what he said, but it was a personal attack that picked apart my status as a psychologist early in her career. His tirade made me feel small, incompetent, and, if I'm honest, more than a little scared. I remember my heart thudding in my chest and the adrenaline coursing through my body, seemingly paralyzing my ability to respond. Maya Angelou says, 'People will forget what you said, people will forget what you did, but people will never forget how you made them feel.' I remember how he made me feel that day.

However, in reflecting on this experience almost 20 years later, I am now struck by one question: What feelings had I drawn out in him? Along with my co-facilitator, the group program that asked for the offence account, and a system that required people to do this type of work in order to move through it, I had compelled him to confront his feelings of shame – and I had compelled him to do so when witnessed by others. It had simply been too much shame for him and he had defended himself against it. And how had he done that? By shaming me right back.

Today, I look back on this experience with new eyes. Of course, I still think it was crucial for the men in the program to understand the factors that had led them to offend. Of course, it's important that opportunities to receive treatment are offered. However, I now question whether activating shame in the way the work did for this particular man was helpful. I was young and inexperienced then and simply doing my job as I'd been asked to do it. Today, I understand the importance of feeling safe enough to get to the root of shame. This man didn't feel safe and he couldn't access his shame as a consequence.

For the majority of you reading this book, of course, the source of your shame is unlikely to be criminal offending. It may well be the things you have done or ways in which you've behaved, but it may also be experiences you've had that were not under your control. Regardless of the source of your shame, feeling it – really feeling it – is your passport to freedom.

Shifting Shame and Self-Talk

Shifting shame is not something that we achieve simply by focusing on our mind alone. It needs to be active and behavioral, too. To release ourselves from shame's steely grip, we must make a conscious choice each time we talk to ourselves without kindness or catch ourselves in shameful self-reproach.

Many times, I've been asked by clients how to let go of the shame they feel. My answer: through the right conditions and making the choice to do exactly that. I know it seems simplistic. It may even feel dismissive, but it's not intended to be. Let me explain further. It doesn't matter how many self-development books you read or how much therapeutic work you do, if your internal self-talk is negative and you're continually telling yourself that you are a useless, worthless, or bad person, the shame that underlies these core beliefs will not lift. And make no mistake, your continuing negative self-talk is a choice you are making. If you're not actively working to release shame, but passively allowing it to remain, it will not lift. But what does it mean to be 'active' in the work?

Activating the Micro-Moments

In therapy, it's crucial to slow things down. People are often looking for the quick fix, and neglect important aspects of their emotional state in the rush to arrive at a solution. Slowing things down instead offers an opportunity to identify what I call the micro-moments – the moments in which we can intervene and change how we view and think about things, and consequently how we feel and respond to them.

An example of this might be feeling aggrieved at something your partner has said or done. However, rather than responding immediately to that angry feeling, you might intervene by allowing yourself the time to attune to the feeling for a few moments first. This offers you the chance to understand more effectively the 'why' of your emotional reaction (perhaps you felt criticized) and then respond more appropriately to it by communicating that feeling to your partner. Slowing things down and activating the micro-moments in this way allows us to attune to our emotional state, and consider how our emotions can often be in the driving seat. Just what are you really feeling right now, in this moment? And now?

Healthy emotional attunement is crucial at this stage of your healing journey, because without it you will be missing a fundamental piece of the puzzle that allows you to know how to intervene and change the story.

The Practice of Non-Attachment

Anecdotally, the people who are most successful in therapy are those who learn and apply the hard lesson of letting things go. Rather than allowing our thoughts or actions to become an extension of us, we must separate them from who we are as people.

Our thoughts and actions are not us, and we are not our thoughts or our actions.

Let me be clear, this does not mean taking no responsibility for the things we've done that perhaps we had rather we hadn't. It simply means accepting that we are not what we think or what we do. You are not your hasty actions or impulsive mistakes. You are not the one-night stand, or that heated argument with your sibling. You are not the disagreements you've had with your partner or children. You are not your depression or anxiety. You are not your eating disorder, past misdemeanors, or failed relationship. Your worth cannot be defined by any of these things. This is what we mean by nonattachment.

The practice of nonattachment for me has been the realization that my worth is ever-present and not dependent on whether I've met my own high expectations or fallen short of them. While writing this chapter of the book, I crashed my car on the way to work one morning. I won't go into the specifics, but ultimately I was deemed 'at fault' by my insurer. Even the language of that feels hard for me to acknowledge as a 'play by the rules' type of person. I felt terrible for the other driver, who had been going about their day unwittingly before my actions impacted them, quite literally. The accident has meant I've had to make arrangements that have involved asking for and accepting help from others, and there will be additional consequences going forward, too. In these circumstances, it would have been very easy to berate myself and to continue to pick fault with my actions. But what good would that have done?

I know that my worth as a person is neither defined nor diminished by what happened that morning. My worth was present before, during, and after the event. I was able to view it as an opportunity to practice some gratitude for how the collision happened. Thankfully, no one was seriously hurt. We were able to move off the road safely and seek assistance, and I was offered kindness and compassion not only by the driver of the other car, but from people who had witnessed the incident. That, of course, has made it easier for me to hold on to the notion of my identity as a good and well-intentioned person who didn't set out that morning to create strife. After the initial shock of the collision, I was able to take responsibility for my part in what had happened – and to show myself compassion as I navigated what came next.

I realized there was a message within what had happened about the things I might consider changing to feel more present and regulated as I get inside my car each morning to drive it. However, I rejected the internal pressure to attach myself to this event and see it as evidence that I was a 'bad' person.

It may seem strange to put it like this, but, all in all, I feel good about how I dealt with this unforeseen situation. It's a mistake that I am putting right, but not something that I will allow to derail me from who I know myself to be. These days, that is never up for negotiation. Life is constantly giving us opportunities to do the work and show up for ourselves in powerful ways, and this was one of them for me.

Over the many years of my clinical practice, I've seen how shame, more than any other emotion, has the unique power to silence people, preventing them from seeking the support they need. As a construct, shame is essentially the belief that at your core you are intrinsically bad – and I want to allow you to let that belief go. The way you are going to do this is by cultivating compassion. Sounds simple, doesn't it, and in many ways it is. But simple does not always mean easy....

What Is Compassion?

According to the online *Merriam-Webster* dictionary, compassion is 'the sympathetic consciousness of others' distress together with a desire to relieve it.' My wish is for you to take this approach to your own distress, too, by developing self-compassion.

In recent years, therapies that focus on compassion have multiplied and become a core part of the therapeutic zeitgeist. Professional psychological therapies aside, an online search using the term 'compassion' yields hundreds of thousands of posts and online video content on the topic. Today, compassion focused therapy (CFT) is one of the core psychological therapies used within the therapeutic space. It was founded by the British clinical psychologist Paul Gilbert, when he realized that people who lived with high levels of shame and self-criticism found it challenging to generate a kind and self-supporting inner dialogue when engaging in therapy (Gilbert, 2009).

Makes sense. If you're someone who feels shameful and you're highly self-critical, then you will find it difficult to talk to yourself with kindness or take a compassionate approach to your mistakes. In schema therapy, we term this kind of harsh self-talk your 'inner critic mode.' When your inner critic is strong, you'll naturally be exposed to more shame, self-blame, and internal distress. Invariably, you'll find it harder to contain your emotional experience, and you will be more prone to either ignoring or invalidating your own needs, and be less able to execute strategies for effective self-soothing. (Within the context of psychology, self-soothing refers to any behaviors that help regulate our nervous systems and emotional state; *see page 176 for more on this.*)

Professor Gilbert takes a biopsychosocial approach, which I once had the pleasure of hearing him discuss in person, when he visited the hospital department in which I worked. I remember being struck by the highly evolutionary basis of compassion, as he described it. In evolutionary terms, he explained, compassion allowed primitive societies to operate well and thrive. We needed compassion to build relationships and maintain them, and having a network of compassionate others ensured a higher probable survival rate.

His research has also highlighted important relationships between compassion and neurology, neurophysiology, genetics, and endocrinology, as well as how our relationships and socio-cultural environments can influence our experience and expression of compassion (Gilbert, 2009, 2014). It almost seems to go without saying that the societies and cultures in which we exist today will similarly influence our own capacity for compassion. Given that the research seems to suggest that a village setting provides the optimum context within which to promote and cultivate compassion, I find it interesting that cultural shifts over time have reduced our perceived need for 'the village.' Though we find ourselves in some respects in a more accessible world than ever before, I believe that our capacity for compassion today has inevitably been reduced by the disconnection caused by, for example, social media and the global pandemic.

If we were to take Gilbert's findings and apply them to the sort of work we're doing in this book, we could similarly say that our individual relationships and how they function will have been shaped by what we were modeled around compassion in our early years. For example, if you can now see that your primary caregiver was not particularly self-compassionate, then it's likely that the types of behaviors that underpin self-compassion will not be particularly familiar to you, because you simply didn't see them in operation.

How Can You Cultivate Self-Compassion?

Though developing self-compassion may sound vague, idealistic, or even a bit 'soft,' this is not the passive technique you might think. Kristen Neff, an associate professor at the University of Texas, talks of three core components to cultivating self-compassion (Neff, 2009). Each one of these components requires active engagement in order to be effective.

The first of these is self-kindness, which involves treating ourselves kindly, with empathy over judgment. Taking a nonjudgmental stance is central to my role as a therapist, and it makes complete sense to me that developing self-compassion asks us to offer ourselves the same sort of qualities that we might receive within the therapeutic relationship or loving familial relationship – things like encouragement, patience, and gentleness. If therapy offers a reassuring and soothing reciprocity of relationship, then that is what you're trying to cultivate in terms of how you treat yourself.

The second component is about recognizing that we share a common humanity; and with that common humanity comes the recognition that we're imperfect – and others are too.

The final component of compassion is mindfulness, which is essentially about sitting with what is true for us in the present moment. To be able to show ourselves compassion, we first need to acknowledge the suffering we're going through, but this can be difficult when our emotional suffering is actually perpetuated by our own inner critical voice. This component is therefore about allowing ourselves to notice our difficult emotions just as they are, the role we have in creating our own suffering, and knowing that the emotions will soon pass – all of which will allow us to offer ourselves compassion.

Let's consider each of these component parts in turn and how you might begin to start working on incorporating them into your life.

Self-Kindness through Self-Soothing

If self-kindness is about treating ourselves in the way that we might treat a friend or someone we love, then acknowledging and soothing distress through kind words and actions is key. Engaging in self-soothing activities to regulate your emotional state is a habit that I want you to develop, going forward.

Self-soothing is often talked about within the context of infant mental health. Even very young babies demonstrate self-soothing behaviors such as sucking or the use of touch, and helping small children to learn strategies to soothe themselves when distressed is a common goal of parenting. As parents, we scaffold our children's learning by showing them first through what we do, encouraging them to try it for themselves, and then, over time, they assimilate the new self-soothing behavior into their own repertoire.

However, if you never received any modeling for self-soothing, the chances are you might struggle with your own emotional regulation in adulthood. When challenging events happen in your life, you might find containing the distress you feel a challenge. Perhaps you saw your parents unable to contain their own negative emotions and lacking any self-soothing strategies to deploy in stressful situations.

Being unable to self-soothe can lead to all sorts of unhelpful behaviors in adulthood, such as seeking excessive reassurance and over-dependency on others for emotional containment and comfort. It's therefore helpful to consider how good you are currently at self-soothing and to consider expanding your repertoire if you find it to be limited.

Of course, what is soothing for one person might be quite the opposite for someone else! The nature of self-soothing is often highly individual and subject to nuance and gradation. People's preferences might also be influenced by sensory sensitivities and what feels familiar or pleasurable. Self-soothing behaviors can be as simple as drinking a warm cup of tea under a cozy blanket, or taking part in a mindful activity or meditation. It could be holding your partner's hand, sharing your feelings with a friend, or reading a book while taking a bath. In the exercise at the end of this chapter, you'll have a chance to identify the self-soothing behaviors that currently work for you and to add some more strategies to that list.

In our family, touch is something that my children seek often and are familiar with, whether that be in the form of a cuddle or simply by sitting close to me on the sofa. They also love a massage. For them, touch is highly regulating. That won't be the case for all children, of course. However, I find that when my children are struggling with their emotional response to something, simply getting down on my hands and knees to offer a cuddle can be enough to bring them back within their personal window of tolerance.

We have even developed special language around it. If my boys ask for one of 'those' cuddles at bedtime, they mean one in which I scoop them up, their head resting on my chest, and rock them for a few minutes. It feels like the type of interaction you would have with an infant and my boys are not babies anymore. But, in asking for one of 'those' cuddles, they have learned to ask for what they know instinctively that they need. They will store the bodily memory of this, and remember in the future that touch helps to soothe them. They are learning to trust that their needs will be met by me, and by extension by others, as they grow and become adults themselves.

You Are Not Perfect

When I first learned that compassion is supported by the acceptance that we are not perfect, it was music to my ears. Earlier in this book, I've mentioned my own struggles with perfectionism, yet I hadn't ever been told I was a perfectionist, nor that it was a problem for me, until a clinical supervisor raised it in one of our regular supervision sessions. She was very matter-of-fact about it, but at the time, I was quite threatened by her observation and I remember feeling very exposed and found out.

She had noticed that I kept putting off writing a report that I'd been asked to do. Her view was that the report wasn't a big deal. Nothing to be concerned about. My view was it was an incredibly big deal and I didn't want to get it wrong. So, I simply hadn't started it – over and over again – for fear of failure. In schema terms, my 'perfectionistic over-controller' mode had taken command and was trying to protect me from criticism by doing nothing at all. But the criticism came anyway.

Despite a highly experienced clinician telling me what she believed, I still didn't face the reality of my perfectionism fully. I think, back then, I believed perfectionism was characterized by always getting things in on time and looking like A+ material, when in fact perfectionism can compel some of us to procrastinate and avoid things. And though I was a perfectionist, I still made mistakes, and that can feel confusing. We may assume that perfectionists actually are perfect in all they do. That obviously isn't true, because nobody can possibly be perfect in everything.

The headline is this: I am not perfect, far from it. And neither are you. But more than that, you're not supposed to be.

Isn't that a relief? I know it is for me. And when we can finally understand how imperfection is part of living a full life, we can just go about living it, trying our best, and giving ourselves the grace and space we need when we are flawed and when we fail. Which is likely to be often.

Sitting with Your Emotions

The third component of self-compassion is about your ability to sit with difficult emotions. Mindfulness asks us to allow our emotions to pass like clouds traveling across a blue sky – without identification. They are there and we acknowledge them, but we are not attached to them and they are not us. So much of what I see clinically are patterns of expectation and harsh self-criticism driven by the self. If we can learn through developing a mindfulness practice that our emotions will not destroy us and that we have control over the inner self-talk that drives our negative emotions, then we have a very good chance of reducing our psychological suffering.

Before you complete this chapter, I want you to sit for a while and consider the impact shame has had on you across your life, and how you might begin to cultivate more compassion to counteract it. Essentially, what are the things you need to do or change to cultivate greater self-compassion and 'treat' the unresolved shame that may have kept you stuck?

COMPASSION PRESCRIPTION QUESTIONS

The following questions are designed to help you consider the role of shame in your life and then develop your own 'compassion prescription,' using the three components of compassion:

Shame

- *What has been your experience of shame throughout your life? Spend some time reflecting and writing on this.*

- *Did any particular memories come up for you, and what have you understood about the impact of shame on your life?*

- *What do you now understand about ways you have blocked self-compassion?*

Self-kindness and self-soothing

- *In what ways might you show yourself more kindness, going forward?*

- *What can you incorporate into your life that will help you to self-soothe when you are distressed?*

- *How can you ensure you remain 'active' in this on an ongoing basis?*

Recognizing and embracing imperfection

- *Have you previously held yourself to high standards that have been unattainable?*

- *How might you begin to allow yourself the grace and space to be imperfect?*

- *How might accepting the imperfection of self and others benefit you?*

Mindfulness and emotions

- *How can you incorporate more mindfulness of your emotional suffering into your life?*

- *In which ways are you your own harshest critic?*

- *How can you better notice and limit your self-criticism to reduce your negative emotional experiences?*

CHAPTER 9

Powerfully Imperfect Living: A Holistic Perspective

Many times, in my professional life, I've been asked by clients to tell them what they need to do to 'fix' whatever problems they face. Consequently, one of the most prominent parts of my job is having hard conversations and tempering these expectations with a healthy dose of reality. 'Fixing' is not really what I do. The past cannot be fixed or cease to exist. It simply is, in the same way that Matty died and that reality is simply what is.

I, of course, don't do any fixing anyway for my clients or for you, the reader. The responsibility for that part belongs solely to you. I can talk and help you understand. I can facilitate, guide, and hold your hand to some extent. But the work is yours to do.

In the end, it always comes back to
what you yourself are going to do
to 'fix' the issues that you face.

That is the focus of this last chapter. I want you to finish reading with a sense of what you are going to do about your situation. For me, therapy should always be active and engaged. What does your new understanding of yourself and your awareness of the past mean? What message does it offer in terms of the changes you need to make and the way you will choose to live your life, going forward? This chapter offers you an opportunity now to plan the 'treatment' you require. How will you 'treat' yourself? And how will you expect others to 'treat' you? This will become your plan for future living.

From Formulation to Holistic Treatment

In psychology, I think it's fair to say that we have been on a journey in terms of how we 'treat' patients. For a long time, the mind was considered as a separate entity from the body and separate, too, from the societies and cultures in which it existed. This view has changed gradually alongside the growing evidence base and the recognition by patients and clinicians of the intrinsic links and influence of the brain on the body, and the body on the brain.

Inevitably, the communities, societies, and cultures in which we exist have an influence on our health and well-being. The extent to which these structures validate or invalidate those past experiences that have had an impact on our mental health is important.

This is why it's crucial to work holistically,
incorporating an understanding of
our internal and external realities.

We need to approach the 'doing' of therapy while considering the mind, body, and soul, as well as the collective community and societal influences.

When you have done the work of understanding your own psychological story – what the difficulties are and where they have arisen from – you will be able to do two things. The first is that you will be able to link your past experiences to your current difficulties. If you can't do this yet, you need to revisit Chapter 7 and consider your formulation, as otherwise you won't know what the 'treatment' needs to look like to resolve it. The second thing is that once armed with that knowledge, you can extrapolate what the unmet need is. Essentially, the past experience offers an insight into the current difficulty, from which you can extrapolate what need you are meeting from behaving in certain (usually unhelpful) ways, and consequently how you can meet that same need in healthier ways.

Let me give you an example in the form of a brief mini-formulation that illustrates the types of links you're trying to make in your own psychological work. Let's say that in your childhood there was a lot of uncertainty and a lack of emotional safety. Life often felt chaotic and out of control. When you find yourself during a period of work stress as an adult, these feelings of lacking safety and stability arise, and create discomfort and a degree of distress.

You develop a coping strategy of restricting your food consumption, as you feel it's one area that allows you to exert conscious control over your life. Though perhaps you don't notice it at first, you begin to lose weight, and you notice an impact on your patience at home and on feelings of closeness with your partner. These are the 'presenting problems' and the unmet need is that of feeling safe.

Knowing this, you choose to treat yourself by sharing what is happening for you with your partner. This immediately helps you to feel safer, as your partner can now share in your struggle and offer support around mealtimes, as you choose to resume a more normal eating pattern. This helps you to develop feelings of closeness to your partner and increases your tolerance of challenges at home. Going forward, you know that when you feel unsafe, this is a trigger that can lead to maladaptive coping and is something that you'll need to pay close attention to.

The Anxious or Depressed Mind

As our previous example illustrates, beneath the symptoms that people present with when they feel broken, underlying relational problems can often be found when we dig deeper. In the same way, the anxious or depressed mind is a symptom and consequence of what lies beneath. In fact, two of the most common psychological disorders are typically anxiety and depression, and many people reading this book may have experienced the symptoms of these problems before. And, of course, anxiety and depression often present alongside other psychological disorders, including phobias, obsessive compulsive disorder, and eating disorders.

So let's think about each of them in turn, in the hope that fostering a deeper relational understanding will help you to keep any symptoms at bay, as you become better equipped to deploy individualized strategies and are more able to notice when your own psychological vulnerabilities are triggered.

What to Do When You're Anxious

My clinical experience of those who are anxious is that once anxiety has taken hold, it is avoidance that maintains it. Whether that anxiety is of a social nature, generalized, or a simple phobia, avoidance is a core feature that keeps us stuck in a holding pattern. And the treatment for this is typically exposure. Whatever it is driving the fear and anxiety, it must be faced.

If this describes you, then to be successful in reducing your symptoms you will need to explore the root of the anxiety and begin to walk toward it, instead of turning in the other direction. The point of exposure work as a treatment is to allow you to learn that you can do scary and hard things, and though your anxiety will increase initially, it will then peak, plateau, and begin to dissipate over time. Providing that you continue to expose yourself to that which caused you anxiety in the first place, you can influence change and reduce the anxiety you feel to manageable levels in a process called extinction.

What to Do When You Feel Depressed

With depression, the challenge is slightly different. If left untreated, anxiety sometimes leads us down a path that means we become more limited and isolated in our life as time goes on. We avoid so many things that, over time, we become disconnected from both ourselves and others. This can, in turn, affect our mood and motivation, and lead to depression. However, depression can of course also arise on its own.

A depressed mind is one that has lost interest in things. If you've experienced this, you might know how previously simple tasks like brushing your teeth or having a shower can feel impossible.

Depression can further isolate us, as we struggle to maintain friendships and our social networks. Life can become shades of grey and we find ourselves doing little, further compounding our low mood.

To treat depression, we need to get back to basics and essentially kick-start ourselves from inaction to action. In clinical psychology, we call this approach 'behavioral activation.' It can often be helpful when your mood is low, because it works on the premise that simple tasks build on your opportunities for success and mastery, boost your mood, and lead in turn to increased motivation to do more things, which leads to even bigger gains in our well-being. It's also worth saying that I've seen clinically how CBT sometimes doesn't work well when a client's mood is very low, because their cognition can be quite impaired. This is when behavioral activation can be most helpful.

If there is a pattern, or particular type of 'mind' that I'm most prone to, it's an anxious one. I wonder whether you know what it is for you, after reading this?

> Knowing the basic approaches
> to begin to 'treat' these things for
> yourself will start you on the path.

If you're feeling anxious, you will need to lean in and do the thing. If you're feeling depressed, try to get back to doing the basics and build from there. Of course, a book cannot provide the nuance and detail on how you plan to approach your difficulties. Only you can do that.

And just in case you didn't read the introduction at the beginning of the book, I need you to understand something. Self-help work is powerful. It is a valid and important part of healing ourselves psychologically. But it may not be for everyone. Or it may not be for you yet, or at this particular time. Doing the work suggested in this book is not a substitute for therapy with a trained mental health professional. But if you do it, it will offer you a platform upon which to build. I hope that will empower you to take the next step and then the one after that.

What to Do When You Feel Broken

By now, you will have likely understood that I am what you could call an eclectic practitioner. Many clinical psychologists are. It helps us to be able to draw on different models and therapies that tap into different types of psychopathologies. My practice, and the complexity of patients I work with, require an eclectic mix of approaches. This allows for a truly individualized experience of therapy and the benefits it can bring.

Within this book you have heard about a variety of therapies, including cognitive behavioral therapy (CBT), cognitive-analytical therapy (CAT), schema therapy, and compassion focused therapy (CFT). There are of course many more. But in the end, no matter what the modality, I believe that therapies are all pointing toward the same fundamental truth: When we feel broken, we need to find ways to put ourselves back together. Piece by piece, we must integrate our parts, heal, and understand how and why we relate to ourselves as we do.

In the years since losing Matty, I've worked hard to embrace a method that allows me to do that. Alongside my own understanding of my psychological 'story,' I've come back time and time again to the power of imperfect living. My life can never now be free of grief. I can never know the freedom and peace of mind of my life before. It is imperfect.

That once 'perfect to us' vision of what our life could have been has gone.

Broken. But I still want to live fully. I have a desire for my children to live fully, too.

And so, 'powerfully imperfect living' was born. It's not a treatment or a therapy. It has become a concept that I see as pivotal to fostering a positive relationship with myself and to making sense of a loss that was nonsensical. It's a way of being and of going about my life. And though it's not a formal treatment or approach, it is rooted in the evidence I've gathered over my career for how to live and function as best I can psychologically.

If my clinical practice and spousal loss have taught me anything, it's that challenging things happen to good people, and I've met many good people on my journey to this point. I've met good people imprisoned for the ways in which they've coped with their challenging circumstances. But that was their behavior, not who they are. All of us deserve a chance to feel whole again after whatever trauma we have faced across our lifetime. When I felt broken, powerfully imperfect living became my philosophy for living.

What Is Powerfully Imperfect Living?

At the core of the philosophy of powerfully imperfect living lies the concept of meeting your unmet needs. Whether you are considering what to do when you feel anxious, depressed, or broken, at the core of this you are likely to find unmet needs. Meeting our unmet needs can be hard. The reality is that busy and perhaps even chaotic lives make it a difficult premise to stick to. However, if you are serious about changing things, then this is one way in which you can go about it.

For me, living powerfully and imperfectly has involved many different things related to meeting my needs. It has been about finding love again with my partner, who also lost his spouse. It has been knowing there is no set timeline on grief and new love; no appropriate number of months to avoid people's judgments of my decision. I met my need for relatedness.

It's been about accepting the forced changes that came into my life, and allowing my anger and frustration around that to be worked through and processed. I met my need for inner peace.

It's been about realizing how precious our lives really are and living with that at the forefront of my mind each and every day. It's been about making powerful and empowered decisions to do new and scary things. I met my need for autonomy. It's been about dreaming that one day I would write a book that might help other people heal.

> The beauty of this philosophy is that
> you can make it whatever you want.

What does living powerfully mean to you? What does living imperfectly mean to you? Hold these questions in mind as you move on to the next section, which will set you up to complete your own needs-based assessment. It will introduce you to a model that I often find helpful to clients. This model will form the basis of the last piece of work I want you to complete, which involves a needs-based assessment where you will consider your own specific needs across the 11 domains within this model, and how you can begin to live differently.

The Good Lives Model

The Good Lives Model (GLM) offers an insightful perspective on the core human needs that need to be met if we are to feel fulfilled and have a good life (Ward and Mann, 2004). Though this model was originally developed in psychological work with offenders, the applications are wide-reaching.

I first used the model myself within a prison-based context. At the time, we were using it to consider the unmet needs of the men who attended our rehabilitation groups. It provided an incredibly helpful framework for looking back and ascertaining which of their needs were unmet before they offended, and also how they might better meet their needs on their release. The premise within the context of the criminal justice system was that if the men's needs were not met in any of the 11 domains described by the model, this made it more likely that they would seek to meet their needs through offending behavior in the future.

Now, clearly this book is not aimed at those who have previously offended, but let's explore this for a moment with an example. Let's assume that your needs have previously been unmet in the domain of pleasure and feeling good in the here and now. In the past, you have used alcohol to activate feelings of pleasure. It provided a near immediate dopamine hit. Over time, perhaps that became problematic for you, as you realized drinking was causing you to feel sluggish and impatient. Now you're armed with that knowledge, you can identify other ways to meet your need for pleasure in the moment in a healthier way. The diagram on page 194, describes the Ward and Mann model and I would like you to use it to inform your personal needs-based assessment in the final exercise.

I will use myself as another example. If I consider how I felt in the immediate aftermath of Matty's death, there was no inner sense of peace. Instead, that had been replaced with mental turmoil. I had lost the man I had chosen to live with for the rest of my life, and one of the most important relational connections I had was now severed. I questioned not a god but a universe that would allow him to be taken from us. It felt like our family had been singled out for tragedy and I was so very angry about that.

I would often see couples and question the fairness of my family's new reality in comparison to theirs. I rarely felt good and spent much of my time at home alone, always putting my children's needs and the needs of others before my own. I was disconnected from my community, my colleagues, and even my friends, who I believed couldn't understand, no matter how hard they tried, what this felt like. If we relate this to the concept of unmet needs, it was clear that the things I required to live 'a good life' were simply not present.

Though I wasn't conscious of it, I slowly began to address the lack of these things in my life. Over time, I was gradually able to meet my needs for relatedness and inner peace; I took up new hobbies and interests, and I found meaning and purpose, defined as spirituality in this model. Interestingly, 'finding meaning' is a core element of Elisabeth Kübler-Ross's 'stages of grief' model, too.

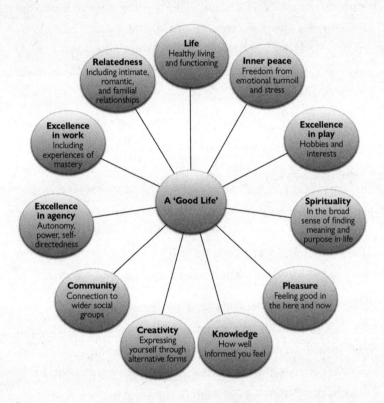

The Good Lives Model/Ward and Mann

And I know that these principles can be applied to your life as well. The Good Lives Model will allow you to consider how your needs are being met across the 11 domains right now, and how you might look to meet them in the future you're seeking to create for yourself.

YOUR HOLISTIC NEEDS ASSESSMENT

In this final exercise of the book, we will use the framework offered by the Good Lives Model and the individual components of what makes a good life. I would like for you to consider and journal on these components, now and where you might like these to be in one year from now, within each of the domains.

Domain 1: Life (Healthy living and functioning)

- *Current assessment: To what extent are your needs met in this domain currently?*

- *Future assessment: How might you like these needs to be met one year from today?*

- *Action steps: What do you need to do to make that future vision a reality?*

Domain 2: Inner peace (Freedom from emotional turmoil and stress)

- *Current assessment: To what extent are your needs met in this domain currently?*

- *Future assessment: How might you like these needs to be met one year from today?*

- *Action steps: What do you need to do to make that future vision a reality?*

Domain 3: Excellence in play (Hobbies and interests)

- *Current assessment: To what extent are your needs met in this domain currently?*

- *Future assessment: How might you like these needs to be met one year from today?*

- *Action steps: What do you need to do to make that future vision a reality?*

Domain 4: Spirituality (In the broad sense of finding meaning and purpose in life)

- *Current assessment: To what extent are your needs met in this domain currently?*

- *Future assessment: How might you like these needs to be met one year from today?*

- *Action steps: What do you need to do to make that future vision a reality?*

Domain 5: Pleasure (Feeling good in the here and now)

- *Current assessment: To what extent are your needs met in this domain currently?*

- *Future assessment: How might you like these needs to be met one year from today?*

- *Action steps: What do you need to do to make that future vision a reality?*

Domain 6: Knowledge (How well informed you feel)

- *Current assessment: To what extent are your needs met in this domain currently?*

- *Future assessment: How might you like these needs to be met one year from today?*

- *Action steps: What do you need to do to make that future vision a reality?*

Domain 7: Creativity (Expressing yourself through alternative forms)

- *Current assessment: To what extent are your needs met in this domain currently?*

- *Future assessment: How might you like these needs to be met one year from today?*

- *Action steps: What do you need to do to make that future vision a reality?*

Domain 8: Community (Connection to wider social groups)

- *Current assessment: To what extent are your needs met in this domain currently?*

- *Future assessment: How might you like these needs to be met one year from today?*

- *Action steps: What do you need to do to make that future vision a reality?*

Domain 9: Excellence in agency (Autonomy, power, self-directedness)

- *Current assessment: To what extent are your needs met in this domain currently?*

- *Future assessment: How might you like these needs to be met one year from today?*

- *Action steps: What do you need to do to make that future vision a reality?*

Domain 10: Excellence in work (Including experiences of mastery)

- *Current assessment: To what extent are your needs met in this domain currently?*

- *Future assessment: How might you like these needs to be met one year from today?*

- *Action steps: What do you need to do to make that future vision a reality?*

Domain 11: Relatedness (Including intimate romantic and familial relationships)

- *Current assessment: To what extent are your needs met in this domain currently?*

- *Future assessment: How might you like these needs to be met one year from today?*

- *Action ateps: What do you need to do to make that future vision a reality?*

POWERFULLY IMPERFECT LIVING JOURNAL PROMPTS

Here are some final journal prompts as you consider how you can meet your needs without perfection.

- *How might you embrace living imperfectly?*
- *What would it mean for you to release perfectionism?*
- *How might you live powerfully? What would that look like for you?*

Conclusion:
Riding on the Crest
of a Wave

Late in the summer that my husband died, my mum and dad took us all on a week-long break at a place close to my heart by the North Sea. It was time away from the house where Matty had spoken his last words to us and a welcome reprieve from the relentlessness of grieving.

On the long stretch of white sandy beach, we booked my daughter in to her first surfing lesson. When I checked with the instructor, he said I would need to go into the water with her as she was just five years old, so on the morning of her lesson I dutifully pulled on a damp wetsuit and waded into the bracing surf. My daughter has always been good at most physical activities, so after just 20 minutes the instructor confirmed she was fine on her own under his supervision.

Gently, he encouraged me to go and get a surfboard, and give it a try myself. I was reluctant. It'd been years since I had attempted to surf. On that previous occasion, I hadn't managed to 'pop up' properly and had climbed out of the surf that day feeling like it was a bit of an impossible task. I thought it likely my attempts would go a similar way now and I wouldn't be able to achieve much during one lesson. Finally, however, I grabbed a board, lay flat along its length and paddled out into the inky water, my hands cupped and pushing the seawater through my fingers.

I remember feeling strong as I made my way out into the waves from the beach. The salty spray on my lips, coupled with the sound and feel of the sea, made for a truly sensory experience. For what felt like perhaps the first time since Matty's death, my mind suddenly quietened. The relief I felt was palpable. The relinquishing of control to the sea on which I floated. The blue cold, the salty wet, the sounds all coming together in this intense feeling of moving away from my overactive, sad, and exhausted mind, and back into my body. In his book *Blue Mind* (2018), Dr. Wallace J. Nichols, a marine biologist, wrote about this phenomenon. He describes the 'blue mind' state as 'a mildly meditative state, characterized by calm, peacefulness, unity, and a sense of general happiness and satisfaction with life in the moment.'

After a few pointers from the instructor, I watched a wave swell up behind me and began to paddle, slowly at first and then faster as the wave began to pick up momentum and draw closer. As it lifted the back of my board, I managed to stand. I'm confident it didn't look pretty, but I was up and standing on the crest of that wave.

I felt mildly euphoric as I was carried to shore, smiling. I sensed the energy and speed of the water coursing through me. And then I fell off. I hit the sand with a resounding thud, landing in the clear shallow waters. I couldn't help but think what a metaphor this was for life. Sometimes we are riding high on the crest of a wave and sometimes we fall hard into the depths. Life brings with it joy and suffering, triumph and disaster, light and shade. With life comes death. As I tossed the soaking strands of hair out of my eyes and jumped up, eager to try again, I knew in that moment what it was all for. Life was to be experienced and I was here for it. I was here for all of it.

*

This book was born out of a belief I hold: That psychological knowledge, skills, and access to psychologically informed work should be available to everybody. Unfortunately, when it comes to accessing psychological support, there exists a degree of privilege when it comes to prioritizing who receives therapy, which is often down to who can afford to pay for it. I wanted to offer another, more accessible and, let's be frank, far cheaper way to engage in this type of work.

When I first began searching for a text that would teach the 'how to' of psychological work, ultimately my search came back with reams of textbooks written for clinicians and books that were so heavily leaning in the CBT direction that they often neglected the relational components that I know to be incredibly powerful in facilitating change. So, I set out to write a book that offered an accessible, bank-account friendly, and relational solution to the problem. The contents of this book are meant also to be 'just enough' to teach you what you need to know. The concepts within the book have been intentionally distilled and simplified in order to make it even easier to actually do the work. Not because my audience are unlikely to understand it, but because simple is almost always better. Simple reduces the barriers to actually implementing change and that can only be a good thing.

Now you've read the book, started the work, and prioritized your needs and your emotional well-being, please be proud of yourself. Even if that concept feels alien to you. And remember, this is only the beginning. Psychological work takes time and you will need to give yourself the gift of time for it be effective.

I'm also curious about how you feel right now... I know all too well that when doing self-help work, there can be a sense of getting to the end of a course or trying out the 'latest thing,' only to look around and ask yourself, 'Well, now what?' I want you to resist the temptation to look for the evidence that the contents of the book haven't worked for you or in fact won't. Because, though you may not have seen any evidence of change, it simply might be that the evidence just hasn't shown up – yet! Like all self-help work, you need to apply things consistently and hold out hope for yourself. And if you're not holding out hope for yourself, who is going to do that for you? You owe it to yourself to try to apply the learnings here consistently.

Sometimes, big emotions can break though when we are confronted with our past, so I want you to feel supported as you finish reading. In psychological work, when things are challenging, we might occasionally need to switch from a treatment focus to supportive containment. Supportive containment is exactly what it sounds like: It's about recognizing that your emotions need to be contained before you can move forward in the work. The need for supportive containment is usually indicated when you feel like you're struggling emotionally or there is a sense of overwhelm. Trust that it is all part of the process and pull back slightly if you need to. With your developing skills in emotional attunement, you will begin to recognize these times more easily and accurately, and be able to take the appropriate action.

Offering ourselves supportive containment means giving ourselves the time that we need to process what we've learned and integrate it. It's a bit like making progress one step at a time – climbing up a few stairs and then reaching a plateau where we need to rest a while, as we gather our strength. Think of it as being like scaling a Munro – a Scottish mountain that's over 3,000 feet high. You couldn't possibly tackle the entire climb without breaks along the way to nourish and sustain you. Perhaps now is a time for some supportive containment before you tackle the next step.

The process of writing this book has been a bit like that for me, too. I've written it in fits and starts. At five in the morning and late at night. I've written it during stolen moments throughout my days as a working mum in the blended family that loss built. I've felt guilty for the time away from my children and resentful that I couldn't write any time I wanted to. Every now and then, I've needed to step away to nourish myself and process how the writing itself has shaped my own thinking, and forced me to do even more of this work. Many times, I've slipped into maladaptive coping strategies – avoidance and distraction among them – as my imposter syndrome has reared up. And then I've remembered my love for the written word and found a way back to it again, with the realization that many of the fits and starts actually reflect my underlying psychology: a core belief of never feeling quite good enough or deserving. It's an amusing irony.

Many years ago, as a pupil studying for my Higher in English, my teacher introduced me to Maya Angelou's autobiography,

I Know Why the Caged Bird Sings. Like many who have found her writing, I've loved both her and her work since. Maya was a woman who knew trauma intimately.

While Maya was writing as an American Black woman resisting racist oppression, I like to hope that those that we are 'in relation to' in our own lives are mostly good people and their intention was never to break us.

I saw the teacher who introduced me to Maya's work recently. He was walking slowly down a supermarket aisle as I passed him. He was older and greyer than I remembered, but there was something familiar in his gentle and unhurried demeanor. I remembered how, in soft tones, he was the first person who told me to write what I knew. I was frustrated by this guidance at the time, as an 18-year-old who didn't believe she knew a whole lot.

For a moment, I considered approaching him as he filled his trolley. I followed him furtively for a few moments, taking care to stay out of his line of sight. I felt a bit excited and compelled to tell him that almost 24 years later I had finally taken his advice. I had written about what I knew and was about to become a real-life published writer. I think he'd have gotten a kick out of that. But I never did stop him or speak up. I thought it might embarrass him, or me, or perhaps even look like I was being audacious. Maybe he wouldn't remember me as strongly as I did him.

There it was again. That inner voice that told me to walk on by. That negative self-talk around being a woman willing to stand in her power. That instinct to shrink remains strong – and I suspect that for me, and for many of us, the work will never be done. Perhaps my teacher will read this book one day and recognize himself in my words. Perhaps not. But I will always be grateful to him for bringing Maya's teachings on life and trauma to me.

Her words, particularly in her poem *Still I Rise*, tell us that though life can be unpredictable, there is always certainty in the dawning of a new day and the ending that we welcome each night. She's taught me that no matter what happens next in this life, I can rise still. And so can you.

Endnotes

Chapter 1: Awakening

p.9 In her book *Daring Greatly*, the American author Brené Brown has termed this type of thinking as 'foreboding joy.' For more on this, see Brown, B. (2012), *Daring Greatly*. New York: Penguin Random House, p.117.

p.17 (P)sychological research has long noted the relatedness of perfectionism and obsessive compulsive disorder.... For more on this research, see Frost, R.O. and Steketee, G. (2007), 'Perfectionism in Obsessive-Compulsive Disorder Patients', *Behaviour Research and Therapy*, 35(4): 291–6.

p.18 (E)arly research previously categorized perfectionism as either positive and healthy, or negative and pathological. For more on this, see Hamachek, D.E. (1978), 'Psychodynamics of Normal and Neurotic Perfectionism', *Psychology: A Journal of Human Behavior*, 15(1): 27–33.

p.19 Professor Joachim Stoeber described perfectionism as 'a personality disposition...'. For more on this paper, see Stoeber, J., Haskew, A.E., and Scott, C. (2015), 'Perfectionism and Exam Performance: The Mediating Effect of Task-Approach Goals', *Personality and Individual Differences*, 74: 171–6.

p.19 There are three main types of perfectionism. For more on this, see Hewitt, P.L. and Flett, G.L. (1991), 'Perfectionism in the Self and Social Contexts: Conceptualization, Assessment, and Association with Psychopathology', *Journal of Personality and Social Psychology*, 60(3): 456–70.

p.26 ...shame lies at the heart of why resistance comes up..... For more on this research, see Teyber, E. and Teyber, F. (2010), *Interpersonal Process in Therapy: An Integrative Model.* Boston: Cengage Learning.

p.26 'Rolling with resistance.' For more on this research, see Miller, W.R. and Rollnick, S. (1991), *Motivational Interviewing: Preparing People to Change Addictive Behavior.* New York: Guilford Press.

Chapter 2: Getting to Know Yourself

p.30 Psychological mindedness has been defined as..... For more on this research, see Conte, H. R. and Ratto, R. (1997), 'Self-report measures of psychological mindedness'. In M. McCallum and W.E. Piper (eds.), *Psychological Mindedness: A Contemporary Understanding.* Mahwah, N.J.: Lawrence Erlbaum Associates Publishers, pp.1–26.

p.31 The impaired 'theory of mind'. For more on this research, see Bora, E. and Kose, S. (2016), 'Meta-analysis of Theory of Mind in Anorexia Nervosa and Bulimia Nervosa: A specific Impairment of Cognitive Perspective Taking in Anorexia Nervosa?', *International Journal of Eating Disorders*, 49(8): 739–40.

p.32 Mindfulness is 'the state of being attentive...'. For more on this research, see Brown, K.W. and Ryan, R.M. (2003), 'The Benefits of Being Present: Mindfulness and Its Role in Psychological Well-being', *Journal of Personality and Social Psychology*, 84(4): 822–48.

p.32 (A)n eight-week therapeutic program aimed at stress reduction. For more on this research, see Kabat-Zinn, J. (2020), 'Mindfulness-Based Stress Reduction': https://mbsrtraining.com/mindfulness-based-stress-reduction/ [Accessed 18 October 2024]

p.39 Social learning theory is... all about modeling. For more on this research, see Bandura, A. (1977), *Social Learning Theory.* Englewood Cliffs: Prentice Hall.

Chapter 3: Leaving Old You Behind

p.53 Traumatic loss has been defined as any experience of loss that involves your previously held assumptions of how the world operates. For more on this research, see Kauffman, J. (2002). 'Safety and the assumptive world. In J. Kauffman' (ed.), *Loss of the Assumptive World: A Theory of Traumatic Loss.* New York: Routledge, pp.205–12.

p.53 (T)hese core assumptions are 'shattered' by a traumatic loss. For more on this research, see Janoff-Bulman, R. (1992), *Shattered Assumptions: Towards a New Psychology of Trauma*. New York: Free Press.

p.56 This is known as Beck's Cognitive Triad, after the American psychiatrist Aaron Beck. For more on this research, see Beck, A.T. (1970), 'The Core Problem in Depression: the Cognitive Triad', *Science and Psychoanalysis*, 17:47–55.

p.60 Post-traumatic growth (PTG), first defined by researchers in 1995. For more on this, see Calhoun, L.G. and Tedeschi, R.G. (1999), *Facilitating Posttraumatic Growth: A Clinician's Guide*. Mahwah, NJ: Lawrence Erlbaum Associates; and Calhoun, L.G. and Tedeschi, R.G. (2001), 'Posttraumatic growth: The positive lessons of loss'. In R.A. Neimeyer (ed.), *Meaning Reconstruction and the Experience of Loss*. Washington, D.C.: American Psychological Association, pp.157–72.

p.61 Researchers have also noted that PTG encompasses five key domains. For more on this research, see Tedeschi, R.G. and Calhoun, L.G. (1996), 'The Posttraumatic Growth Inventory: Measuring the positive legacy of trauma', *Journal of Traumatic Stress*, 9(3): 455–71; and Tedeschi, R.G., and Calhoun, L.G. (2004), 'Posttraumatic growth: Conceptual foundations and empirical evidence', *Psychological Inquiry*, 15: 1–18.

Chapter 4: What Makes Us Who We Are

p.67 Bowlby's theory of attachment points out that as infants we are born with an innate set of attachment behaviors. For more on this research, see Bowlby, J. (1969), *Attachment and Loss: Vol. 1. Attachment*. New York: Basic Books; and (1982), 'Attachment and Loss: Retrospect and prospect', *American Journal of Orthopsychiatry*, 52(4): 664–78.

p.71 American psychologist Abraham Maslow, who set out what he believed were basic and core human needs within his five-tier hierarchy of needs model. For more on this research, see Maslow, A. H. (1954), *Motivation and Personality*. New York: Harper & Row Publishers.

p.72 Albert Bandura, a psychologist working out of Stanford University, explained that those working in the field of personality.... For more on this research, see Bandura, A. (1969), 'Social Learning Theory of Identificatory Processes'. In Goslin, D.A. (ed.), *Handbook of Socialisation Theory and Research*. Chicago: Rand McNally.

p.75 ...we now know that certain relational treatments such as Jeff Young's schema therapy.... See Young, J., Klosko, J., and Weishaar, M. (2006), *Schema Therapy: A Practitioner's Guide*. New York: Guilford Press.

Chapter 5: Digging Deeper

p.89 [CBT is] the foundation upon which many other therapies are built. For more on this, see Beck, J. (2020), *Cognitive Behavior Therapy, Third Edition: Basics and Beyond*. New York: Guilford Press.

p.100 [T]he term 'shell-shocked' comes from the reaction of soldiers in World War One. For more on this, see Jones, E. (2012), 'Shell shocked': www.apa.org/monitor/2012/06/shell-shocked [Accessed18 October 2025]

p.103 Reciprocity is a core component of dialectical behavioral therapy, known as DBT. For more on this research, see Linehan, M.M. (1993), *Cognitive-Behavioral Treatment of Borderline Personality Disorder*. New York: Guilford Press.

p.106 I've used this relational mapping process, facilitated by the RRP model from Ryle and Kerr.... For more on this, see Ryle, A. and Kerr, I.B. (2002), *Introducing Cognitive Analytic Therapy: Principles and Practice*. Chichester: John Wiley and Sons.

Chapter 6: Intergenerational Trauma

p.118 In psychology, we use the biopsychosocial model proposed by George L. Engel.... For more on this, see Švorcová J. (2023), 'Transgenerational Epigenetic Inheritance of Traumatic Experience in Mammals'., *Genes*, 14(1): 120; Engel, G. (1977), 'The need for a new medical model: a challenge for biomedicine', *Science*, 196: 129–36.

p.119 Another helpful model to consider in this respect is known as the diathesis-stress model. For an updated view on Paul Meehl's research, see Walker, E.F. and Diforio, D. (1997), 'Schizophrenia: a Neural Diathesis-Stress Model', *Psychological Review*, 104(4): 667.

p.127 Coming from schema therapy, the origins of which were detailed in the book. For more on this research, see Young, J.E. and Klosko, J.S. (1994), *Reinventing Your Life*. New York: Plume.

Chapter 7: Telling Your Own Story

p.139 The original ACEs study looked at the relationship between various categories of traumatic experience and risk behavior, health status and disease. For more on this research, see Felitti, V.J., et al. (1998), 'Relationship of childhood abuse and household dysfunction to many of the leading causes of death in adults: The Adverse Childhood Experiences (ACE) Study', *American Journal of Preventive Medicine*, 14(4): 245–58.

p.148 Psychologists call this an internal working model. For more on this, see Bretherton, I. and Munholland, K. A. (1999), 'Internal working models in attachment relationships: A construct revisited'. In J. Cassidy and P. R. Shaver (eds.), *Handbook of Attachment: Theory, Research, and Clinical Applications*. New York: Guilford Press, pp. 89–111.

p.148 We also know that these models impact our social cognition, emotional regulation.... For more on this research, see Mikulincer, M. and Shaver, P.R. (2016), *Attachment in Adulthood: Structure, Dynamics, and Change* (2nd edition). New York: Guilford Press.

Chapter 8: Releasing Shame and Cultivating Compassion

p.173 [CFT] was founded by the British clinical psychologist Paul Gilbert. For more on this, see Gilbert, P. (2009). 'Introducing Compassion-Focussed Therapy', *Advances in Psychiatric Treatment*, 15, 199–208. For further reading, see Gilbert, P. (2010), *The Compassionate Mind: A New Approach to Life's Challenges*. London: Robinson

p.175 Kristen Neff, an associate professor at the University of Texas. For more, see Neff, K.D. (2009), 'The Role of Self-Compassion in Development: A Healthier Way to Relate to Oneself', *Human Development*, 52(4): 211–14.

Chapter 9: Powerfully Imperfect Living

p.192 The Good Lives Model (GLM) offers an insightful perspective on the core human needs. For more on this research, see Ward, T. and Mann, R. (2004), 'Good Lives and the Rehabilitation of Offenders: A Positive Approach to Treatment'. In P.A. Linley and S. Joseph (eds.), *Positive Psychology in Practice*. Hoboken: John Wiley & Sons, pp.598–616.

p.200 Dr. Wallace J. Nichols, a marine biologist, wrote about this phenomenon. See Nichols, W.J. (2018), *Blue Mind: How Water Makes You Happier, More Connected and Better at What You Do*. London: Hachette.

Resources

Meeting Your Need for Community

You will have read within the book how important connection is for overall healing. For those of you who are new to my world, I would love to offer you the opportunity to join my growing community of people who are doing the work to get to know their psychology better. Join my free Facebook group, Know Your Own Psychology, at the link below:

www.facebook.com/share/bSFzCGkFf6qAqKtw/

Where Else You Can Find Me

www.drlaurawilliams.com

My podcast, Know Your Own Psychology: available on all streaming platforms

Mental Health Resources

Breathing Space (UK): 0800 83 85 87

Samaritans (UK): 116 123

For details of crisis hotlines and resources in the USA, see: www.apa.org/topics/crisis-hotlines

For details of crisis hotlines and resources in Australia, see: www.healthdirect.gov.au/mental-health-helplines

Meditation Resources

Headspace: www.headspace.com

Insight Timer: www.insighttimer.com

Superhuman: www.superhuman.app

Empower You Unlimited Audio: www.empoweryouaudio.com

Acknowledgments

This book would never have been possible without the many people behind me, lifting me up. Firstly, to Michelle Pilley, Reid Tracey, and the rest of the Hay House team. Thank you for seeing something in my writing and giving me the opportunity to tell this story. I will be forever grateful to you.

Special mention to my editors, Lucy Buckroyd and Sue Lascelles. Lucy, you have made what was an unknown and sometimes bewildering process appear simple and straightforward. You were always on hand with a listening ear and a reassuring word. You kept me going when I felt like an imposter and I thank you for your gentle encouragement. Sue, it has been a pleasure to see you take my first draft and skillfully mold and shape it into something better. Cathy Levy, thank you for your expertise and for keeping us on track when it would have been so easy for time to drift.

To my psychology teachers, mentors and colleagues past and present, I thank you for all I have learned from you and all that I am still learning. To my friends and family who have supported me on my book-writing journey, I appreciate you listening to me talk about the book, helping to free up precious time for me to write it, and pushing me to keep going when the juggle felt hard. This was possible because of you. Murray, you have been my most influential cheerleader. You've offered space for my reflections, suggestions when I felt stuck, and, above all, you believed in me. Thank you for being you. To my children, all of you – you are my greatest teachers. Thank you for holding up the mirror and showing me the lessons I must learn.

And to those of you who allowed me to tell your stories within these pages, so that others might benefit, I thank you for your willingness to be vulnerable. Supporting the message of this book, that we are not in fact broken, is an important and valuable contribution.

Finally, to Matty. I hope I've done you proud. X

© Rachel Shootsweet

About the Author

Dr. Laura Williams is a clinical psychologist, trauma therapist, and author. She is also a widow and mum, who put all her psychological expertise into practice when faced with the sudden death of her much-loved husband in 2018. Laura continues to work in the NHS, has contributed to UK-based TV documentaries and print media and hosts the *Know Your Own Psychology* podcast. Laura is passionate about making psychological concepts and information more accessible.

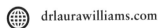 drlaurawilliams.com

 @drlaurawilliams

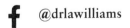 @drlawilliams

 @DoctorLauraWilliams

CONNECT WITH
HAY HOUSE
ONLINE

🌐 hayhouse.co.uk   f @hayhouse

📷 @hayhouseuk   𝕏 @hayhouseuk

▶ @hayhouseuk   ♪ @hayhouseuk

'The gateways to wisdom and knowledge
are always open.'

Louise Hay